How to use your Snap R KU-005-017

This 'Power and Conflict' Snap Revision Guide will help you to get a top mark in the poetry anthology section of your AQA English Literature exam. It is divided into clear sections so you can easily find help with different poems or specific exam skills. This book covers everything you will need to know for the exam:

The poems: a detailed analysis of all fifteen 'Power and Conflict' poems, covering themes, context, poetic voice, and the effects of language, structure, and form.

Comparison: how to come up with ideas and structure a comparison of two poems.

The exam: what kind of questions will come up in the exam, how you can get top marks, and what grade 5 and grade 7+ responses look like.

To help you get ready for your exam, each topic includes:

Key quotations to learn

All the poems from the 'Power and Conflict' anthology are printed in full; useful quotations to memorise are highlighted in pink as these will help you to analyse in the exam and boost your grade.

Additional context to consider

Ideas you can apply to each poem to extend your understanding of how its context has influenced the poet's choices of language, structure, and form.

Poetic links

Details of poems with similar themes or features so you know which ones will work well together in the exam.

Sample analysis

An example of the kind of analysis that the examiner will be looking for.

Quick test

A quick-fire test to check you can remember the main points from the topic.

Exam practice

A short writing task so you can practise analysing each poem.

Glossary

Handy lists of literary terms and general words, with easy-to-understand definitions, that you will find useful when revising the 'Power and Conflict' poetry.

AUTHOR:

IAN

KIRBY

 **ebook**

To access the ebook version of this Snap Revision Text Guide visit

collins.co.uk/ebooks

and follow the step-by-step instructions.

Published by Collins

An imprint of HarperCollins*Publishers*

1 London Bridge Street

London SE1 9GF

HarperCollins*Publishers*

1st Floor, Watermarque Building,

Ringsend Road, Dublin 4, Ireland

© HarperCollins*Publishers* Limited 2018

ISBN 9780008320102

First published 2018

10 9 8 7

British Library Cataloguing in Publication Data.

A CIP record of this book is available from the British Library.

Commissioning Editor: Gillian Bowman

Managing Editor: Craig Balfour

Author: Ian Kirby

Proofreader: Jill Laidlaw

Typesetting: Jouve

Cover designers: Kneath Associates and Sarah Duxbury

Production: Katharine Willard

Printed in the United Kingdom.

ACKNOWLEDGEMENTS

p.31, Seamus Heaney 'Storm on the Island' from Opened Ground by permission of Faber and Faber Ltd; p.35, Ted Hughes 'Bayonet Charge' from Collected Poems by permission of Faber and Faber Ltd; p.39, Simon Armitage 'Remains' from The Not Dead by permission of Pomona; p.43, 'Poppies' by Jane Weir: Copyright Templar Poetry from The Way I Dressed During the Revolution (Templar, 2005); p.47, Carol Ann Duffy 'War Photographer' Copyright © Carol Ann Duffy. Reproduced by permission of Carol Ann Duffy c/o Rogers, Coleridge & White Ltd., 20 Powis Mews, London W11 1JN; p.51, Imtiaz Dharker 'Tissue' reprinted with permission of Bloodaxe Books www.bloodaxebooks.com; p.55, Carol Rumens 'The Émigrée' from Thinking of Skins; p.59, John Agard 'Checking Out Me History' copyright © by John Agard reproduced by kind permission of John Agard c/o Caroline Sheldon Literary Agency Ltd; p.64, 'Kamikaze' by Beatrice Garland: Copyright Templar Poetry from The Invention of Fireworks (Templar, 2013)

The author and publisher are grateful to the copyright holders for permission to use quoted materials and images.

Every effort has been made to trace copyright holders and obtain their permission for the use of copyright material. The author and publisher will gladly receive information enabling them to rectify any error or omission in subsequent editions. All facts are correct at time of going to press.

Contents

OZYMANDIAS by Percy Bysshe Shelley

I met a traveller from an antique land
Who said: Two vast and trunkless legs of stone
Stand in the desert. Near them on the sand,
Half sunk, a shatter'd visage lies, whose frown
5   And wrinkled lip and sneer of cold command
Tell that its sculptor well those passions read
Which yet survive, stamp'd on these lifeless things,
The hand that mock'd them and the heart that fed;
And on the pedestal these words appear:

10   'My name is Ozymandias, king of kings:
Look on my works, ye Mighty, and despair!'
Nothing beside remains. Round the decay
Of that colossal wreck, boundless and bare,
The lone and level sands stretch far away.

This poem is about...

the remains of a statue of an Egyptian **pharaoh**, symbolising how even the most powerful people and the greatest **empires** cannot last forever.

How do the opening lines introduce the theme of power?

The traveller, whose speech is reported by the poem's narrative voice, is from an 'antique' land. This adjective means ancient, thereby establishing the idea of an empire that has now fallen. Although the poem is about an Egyptian pharaoh, Ramesses II, the poet uses the Greek version of the pharaoh's name, allowing the poem to allude to the fall of two great empires.

Important people are often celebrated through statues. In this poem, the statue symbolises the changing nature of Ozymandias's power. It is ironic that this huge symbol of power has now crumbled and collapsed. The pharaoh's former supremacy is conveyed through the adjective 'vast', suggesting enormity and an almost limitless reach, while the noun 'stone' implies strength and endurance.

However, the legs of the statue are 'trunkless' (its body is missing) and the head is 'half sunk' and 'shatter'd'. These adjectives display the loss of Ozymandias's power. Over time, after his death, the empire he built up has been lost. The references to 'the desert' and 'sand' symbolise time and how nothing stays the same.

How do lines 4–8 explore power further?

The description of the ruined face of the statue continues to focus on the pharaoh's power and how it has been lost. Ozymandias is presented as superior and judgemental through the tricolon 'frown / And wrinkled lip and sneer'. The metaphor 'cold command' suggests he was unfeelingly domineering and this is emphasised through the hard sound of the alliterated plosives.

The **duality** of power and loss of power that runs throughout the poem is highlighted in line 7 where Shelley contrasts 'survive' and 'lifeless', showing the pharaoh's greatness only exists as history.

Line 8 can be read in several ways. The 'hand that mock'd them' could continue the idea that the statue is ironic: the sculptor imitated the pharaoh's dominant expression exactly but now it's all that remains of his power. However, it could also suggest that Ozymandias was a bad ruler who did nothing to improve the lives of his people. Similarly, the phrase 'the heart that fed' could suggest that the sculptor, like all the pharaoh's subjects, loved Ozymandias because he built a wealthy nation with plenty of food, or that he was a tyrant who exploited his people to gain greater power and wealth.

What is the significance of the inscription?

Line 9 tells us that the stone legs are on a 'pedestal'. This is the base for a statue and the word is often used as a metaphor for when someone is admired and idolised without any criticism. The first line of the inscription, 'My name is Ozymandias, king of kings', shows the pharaoh's **arrogance** and sense of grandeur in the way that he considers himself above all other rulers. It is also a reference to the growth of his empire, suggesting he has taken control of many other nations.

The second line of the inscription, 'Look on my works, ye Mighty, and despair!', also shows off his power by challenging people to try to surpass his accomplishments ('works'). The verb 'despair' suggests everyone will feel humbled, knowing they cannot outperform him. The capitalisation of 'Mighty' could imply that Ozymandias saw himself as more powerful than God, emphasising the sense of **hubris** that Shelley builds up throughout the poem.

The irony of the inscription is highlighted by the short sentence that follows, 'Nothing beside remains', reminding the reader that all Ozymandias's achievements and power are gone.

What is the message of the final sentence?

The poem ends by highlighting the idea that power isn't eternal, using the nouns 'decay' and 'wreck' to show Ozymandias's loss of greatness. Shelley then returns to the image of sand that he used earlier in the poem to symbolise time. The alliterated pair of adjectives 'boundless and bare' emphasises the idea that nothing now remains of the pharaoh's empire. The similar phrase 'lone and level' draws on the **idiom** that time is a great leveller to suggest that, ultimately, Ozymandias was no different to any of us: he couldn't stop death and he, too, would end up as dust.

How does the poem's form contribute to the way meaning is conveyed?

The poem is written as a sonnet. This traditional form of poetry could be showing respect to Ozymandias or, as the form is often linked to love, could be another representation of the pharaoh's hubris.

The iambic pentameter creates a constant, steady rhythm that could be linked to the poem's theme of unstoppable time.

In the 19th century, lines of poetry were traditionally expected to be end-stopped. However, Shelley uses a lot of enjambment in his poem and creates caesuras by punctuating within the lines. This apparent lack of control (set against the highly structured form of a sonnet) could be another reminder of the limits of Ozymandias's power.

Additional context to consider

The way the poem is told – the narrator reporting somebody's description of the remains of Ozymandias's kingdom – deliberately removes power from Ozymandias. He is placed in the past, described by others, and doesn't get to speak (except for the ironic inscription on the pedestal).

Shelley was part of the Romantic movement and the Romantic poets often rejected the **establishment** and its rules. Shelley's political views were seen as radical in the 1800s: he was critical of the government and **monarchy**, saw power as a corrupting force and believed in greater equality. The poem can be seen as imagining and celebrating the collapse of the establishment.

Poetic links

- Loss of power in 'The Charge of the Light Brigade'.
- Powerful people in 'My Last Duchess' or 'The Prelude'.
- Empire and establishment in 'Checking Out Me History' or 'London'.
- The transience of life in 'Tissue' or 'Exposure'.

Sample analysis

'Ozymandias' and 'Checking Out Me History' both criticise the power of the establishment. Shelley uses the metaphor 'sneer of cold command', when describing the carved image of the pharaoh, to convey the cruelty of rulers. The 'sneer' suggests he looks down on his people, while the adjective 'cold' implies he doesn't care about them. The alliterated plosives emphasise this harsh attitude to others.

Agard also uses metaphor to criticise the establishment but there is a tone of anger as he is critiquing his own society rather than looking back on the past. The line 'Blind me to me own identity' uses a verb with violent connotations to suggest that people are subtly forced to think and feel in a certain way, and that their individuality is not valued. The use of non-standard English represents his retaliation against the establishment.

Questions

QUICK TEST
1. What aspects of the statue show Ozymandias's former power?
2. What aspects of the statue highlight Ozymandias's loss of power?
3. What are the references to sand used to symbolise?
4. In what way is the inscription on the pedestal ironic?

EXAM PRACTICE
Using one or two of the highlighted quotations to learn, write a paragraph exploring how Shelley presents a loss of power.

LONDON by William Blake

I wander through each chartered street,
Near where the chartered Thames does flow,
And mark in every face I meet
Marks of weakness, marks of woe.

5 In every cry of every man,
In every infant's cry of fear,
In every voice, in every ban,
The mind-forged manacles I hear:

How the chimney-sweeper's cry
10 Every black'ning church appalls,
And the hapless soldier's sigh
Runs in blood down palace walls.

But most through midnight streets I hear
How the youthful harlot's curse
15 Blasts the new-born infant's tear,
And blights with plagues the marriage hearse.

This poem is about...

the different social problems affecting people in London during the **Industrial Revolution** and how the people in power are to blame.

How does the first stanza establish a critical view of London?

The opening line describes London's 'chartered' streets. Royal charters established cities, boroughs and companies, allocating people ownership and legal rights. Blake saw this as dividing up a country that belonged to everyone. He is criticising the power of the monarchy and different establishments such as the Church, the government and the courts.

He emphasises this by repeating the adjective 'chartered' and relating it to the Thames, creating an image of water (a basic natural resource that should be free to everyone) being divided up among specific people. When the poem was written, towards the end of the 1700s, the Thames was also increasingly polluted by sewage and industrial waste, which the government did nothing to resolve; Blake's allusion to the Thames could also be suggesting that British establishments are dirty and **corrupt**.

Repetition is also used in lines 3 and 4 to introduce the plight of the city's people. 'Mark' is initially used as a verb to show that the speaker is observing London's problems, then as a noun to suggest the physical and emotional damage caused by poverty: 'Marks of weakness, marks of woe.' Alliteration links the two images of unhappiness and suggests that such misery is building up in the city. In the Christian Bible, the story of Passover features the Israelite slaves escaping a great plague by marking their doors with lamb's blood. Blake could be making an allusion to this story, suggesting Londoners are innocent and enslaved.

How does the second stanza show the plight of London's people?

Blake uses anaphora ('In every...') to suggest that everyone in the city is suffering. He depicts the terror of innocent children ('infant's cry of fear') and uses similar language to show that adults are just as weak and vulnerable ('cry of every man').

He uses the noun 'ban' to suggest that freedom has been removed from the people through prohibitive laws. This idea is developed using the powerful metaphor, 'mind-forged manacles', which can be interpreted in several ways. It could suggest that the people are enchained by their own beliefs (a criticism of the Church), that they haven't been taught to value freedom (a criticism of the limited education system) or that they are like slaves and considered less important in the eyes of the people running the country (a criticism of politicians).

What groups of people are presented as victims of the establishment in stanzas 3 and 4?

Blake believed in God but saw the Church as corrupt. Focusing on a child chimney sweeper, he uses a metaphor to accuse the Church of not helping children in poverty: 'cry / Every black'ning church appalls'. Traditional colour symbolism, alluding to chimney soot, links the Church to sin while the verb 'appalls' suggests we should be horrified. Blake also uses wordplay to have the church being covered with a **pall**, implying he wants people to reject the Church and leave it to die.

Another metaphor is used to attack the monarchy for sending soldiers to die in pointless wars. The adjective 'hapless' shows sympathy for soldiers, suggesting they are innocent but doomed. The image 'Runs in blood down palace walls' is also an allusion to the **French Revolution**, implying that the British monarchy will experience the same fate if it does not change.

Blake focuses the final stanza on the city's loss of innocence, hope and goodness, symbolised by the dark ('midnight') setting. He describes a young prostitute ('the youthful harlot') shouting at her baby ('curse / Blasts the new-born infant's tear'), with the verb 'blasts' suggesting anger and aggression. The noun 'curse' has a double meaning: a swear word and a suggestion that this young girl is just as much a victim as her child. It implies this is a vicious circle, due to the lack of social care from the government and the Church, and the baby will also become a prostitute. The final line criticises the **patriarchy** by describing how married men sleep with prostitutes and then pass on venereal diseases ('blights with plagues') to their wives. The metaphor 'the marriage hearse' suggests that ideas of love and family are dying, leaving the future bleak.

How does the poem's form contribute to the way meaning is conveyed?

The first three lines are written in iambic tetrameter and establish the *abab* rhyme scheme. This carefully structured metre and rhyme continues for most of the poem, matching the serious subject as well as reflecting the focus on establishments and restriction.

However, Blake breaks out of this structure to achieve specific effects. When focusing on vulnerable people (lines 9, 11 and 14) or accusing the establishment (lines 4, 10 and 12), he uses trochees instead of iambs. Putting the stressed beat first adds anger and force to Blake's message: MARKS of WEAKness MARKS of WOE. He also removes the last unstressed beat in these lines to give them more power.

Additional context to consider

The narrative voice focuses on different aspects of London in each stanza, as if the reader is accompanying the speaker on a walk around the city.

The focus on the suffering of others, rather than the speaker's own feelings, suggests great sympathy and a desire for change.

Like Shelley ('Ozymandias'), Blake was a Romantic poet. He believed in equality and his criticism of the monarchy, Church and government was quite radical for the time in which he was writing.

Poetic links

- Establishment in 'Ozymandias' or 'Checking Out Me History'.
- The wish to remove power structures in 'Tissue'.
- The effects of power on people and places in 'The Émigrée'.
- Powerlessness in 'The Prelude', 'Exposure' or 'Storm on the Island'.

Sample analysis

'London' and 'The Émigrée' present places as diseased due to misuse of power. Blake ends his poem with the metaphor 'blights with plagues the marriage hearse' to criticise the failings of the state and Church. He uses the noun 'plagues' to suggest that, due to a lack of social reform and charity, a sense of immorality (represented by the 'blights' of venereal disease) is spreading. His use of plosives, falling on the stressed beat of the iambic tetrameter, emphasises his anger at the state of the nation, while the image of the 'marriage hearse' suggests there is no hope for the future.

Rumens uses a similar metaphor of illness, 'it may be sick with tyrants, / but I am branded by an impression of sunlight', to show the effect of corrupt **regimes** on places. Perhaps because, unlike in 'London', the speaker left the place when she was a child and is looking back, her criticisms are juxtaposed with more positive metaphors. The use of 'sunlight' is **nostalgic** but could also symbolise hope for the future.

Questions

QUICK TEST
1. How does Blake use anaphora in the second stanza?
2. What different interpretations could the 'mind-forged manacles' have?
3. How could Blake be seen as warning the Church and the monarchy of the need to change?
4. How is the prostitute presented as a victim?

EXAM PRACTICE
Using one or two of the highlighted quotations to learn, write a paragraph exploring how Blake shows the effect on people of the misuse of power.

THE PRELUDE by William Wordsworth

One summer evening (led by her) I found
A little boat tied to a willow tree
Within a rocky cove, its usual home.
Straight I unloosed her chain, and stepping in
5   Pushed from the shore. It was an act of stealth
And troubled pleasure, nor without the voice
Of mountain-echoes did my boat move on;
Leaving behind her still, on either side,
Small circles glittering idly in the moon,
10 Until they melted all into one track
Of sparkling light. But now, like one who rows,
Proud of his skill, to reach a chosen point
With an unswerving line, I fixed my view
Upon the summit of a craggy ridge,
15 The horizon's utmost boundary; far above
Was nothing but the stars and the grey sky.
She was an elfin pinnace; lustily
I dipped my oars into the silent lake,
And, as I rose upon the stroke, my boat
20 Went heaving through the water like a swan;
When, from behind that craggy steep till then
The horizon's bound, a huge peak, black and huge,
As if with voluntary power instinct,
Upreared its head. I struck and struck again,
25 And growing still in stature the grim shape
Towered up between me and the stars, and still,
For so it seemed, with purpose of its own
And measured motion like a living thing,

Strode after me. With trembling oars I turned,

30 And through the silent water stole my way
Back to the covert of the willow tree;
There in her mooring-place I left my bark, –
And through the meadows homeward went, in grave
And serious mood; but after I had seen

35 That spectacle, for many days, my brain
Worked with a dim and undetermined sense
Of unknown modes of being; o'er my thoughts
There hung a darkness, call it solitude
Or blank desertion. No familiar shapes

40 Remained, no pleasant images of trees,
Of sea or sky, no colours of green fields;
But huge and mighty forms, that do not live
Like living men, moved slowly through the mind
By day, and were a trouble to my dreams.

This poem is about...

the speaker's experience of stealing a boat and rowing across a lake; at first he feels free and powerful but then the scale of the landscape around him makes him feel insignificant and frightened.

How does the opening of the poem set the scene?

The poem is set on a 'summer evening' and Wordsworth creates a peaceful scene. He uses personification to show how quiet and open it is ('the voice / Of mountain-echoes') and describes the lake as beautiful, 'Small circles glittering idly in the moon, / Until they melted all into one track / Of sparkling light'. The verb phrase 'glittering idly', the metaphor 'melted' and the adjective 'sparkling' build up a mood of serenity and contentment.

The speaker suggests a feeling of freedom in the way he found the 'tied' boat and 'unloosed her chain'. By using a feminine pronoun to describe the boat, along with the adjective 'little', the poet also suggests that the speaker feels strong and masculine by taking control of the boat. This is emphasised by his use of the possessive pronoun 'my' to show he controls the boat, as well as the forceful verb in 'Pushed from the shore' and his apparent pride in this 'act of stealth'.

How do lines 11–20 build up the speaker's sense of power?

The caesura in the middle of line 11 creates a dramatic pause that introduces the speaker's boasts about the quality of his rowing: 'But now, like one who rows, / Proud of his skill [...] With an unswerving line'.

Verb phrases are used to convey his strength: 'rose upon the stroke [...] heaving through the water'. His sense of mastery is again conveyed by relating the boat to femininity and smallness, 'She was an **elfin pinnace**', and there could even be a sexual undertone in his choice of language when he says 'lustily / I dipped my oars into the silent lake'. The verb 'dipped' and the adjective 'silent' also suggest that his rowing is impressively graceful and this is emphasised by the simile 'like a swan'.

His sense of power is increased by his feeling that he is all alone and completely free on the lake. He feels like he could keep rowing forever ('the horizon's utmost boundary') and that nothing can hold him back ('far above / Was nothing but the stars and the grey sky'). He also sets himself a target to accomplish, 'I fixed my view', in order to emphasise his power.

How do the speaker's feelings change on lines 21–32?

As the speaker rows towards the horizon, a mountain comes into view. Personification makes the peak sound alive and aggressive: 'huge peak, black and huge, / As if with voluntary power instinct, / Upreared its head'. The repetition of the adjective 'huge' suggests the speaker feels dominated and frightened.

The poet depicts a struggle for power between the speaker and the mountain. While repetition of the verb 'struck' shows the speaker's continued rowing, verbs are also used to suggest the mountain's power, 'growing [...] 'Towered'. The peak's dominance, and the speaker's contrasting weakness and insignificance, is shown by the way it seems to rise up 'between me and the stars', suggesting it is almost godlike. Adjectives show his fear, describing the mountain as 'grim' and admitting his oars are 'trembling'; even the 'silent' waters now suggest danger rather than peace. He turns the boat around and retreats to the shore.

How is the speaker's reaction to the mountain explained at the end of the poem?

The speaker's experience leaves him in a 'grave / And serious mood', thinking of 'unknown modes of being'. The adjectives suggest he has been disturbed by witnessing a power in nature that he didn't realise existed. A metaphor describes his shocked state of mind, 'There hung a darkness, call it solitude / Or blank desertion'.

He felt he was at the centre of his world but was then shown his insignificance. Anaphora is used, 'No familiar shapes / Remained, no pleasant images of trees, / Of sea or sky, no colours of green fields', to show him questioning his place in the world. It could be interpreted as him having seen the power of God in 'huge and mighty forms, that do not live / Like living men', and realising that, in comparison, he is tiny. The final line shows his experience haunts him day and night.

How does the poem's form contribute to the way meaning is conveyed?

'The Prelude' is an extract from a longer autobiographical poem. It is an example of lyric poetry as it expresses powerful personal emotions.

The poem is written in blank verse. The lack of rhyme could reflect the poet's initial feelings of freedom, while the steady iambic pentameter portrays his sense of strength and power, as well as the steady rhythm of the rowing.

Additional context to consider

The poem is autobiographical, describing a real experience. The use of **first person**, plus the fact he is alone, increases the poem's immediacy and intimacy.

Wordsworth was a Romantic poet and one of their key themes was the power and importance of nature.

Poetic links

- Sources of power in 'Ozymandias' or 'My Last Duchess'.
- Powerlessness in 'London'.
- The power of nature in 'Exposure' or 'Storm on the Island'.

Sample analysis

'The Prelude' and 'London' both present people's powerlessness. Perhaps because it is an autobiographical poem, Wordsworth focuses on his personal feelings of powerlessness when he witnesses the forces of nature. Personifying the mountain, he describes how it 'Towered up between me and the stars', using the verb to convey a sense of dominance. It is presented as physically restricting the speaker and the reference to the 'stars' implies it is almost godlike.

In contrast, Blake focuses on the powerlessness of others, describing 'Marks of weakness, marks of woe' in the faces of the Londoners that he sees. The alliteration of 'weakness' and 'woe' connects the two abstract nouns to imply that such misery is building up across the city, while the repetition of 'marks' presents the people as physically damaged. Blake may also be making an allusion to the story of the Passover, linking Londoners to the Israelites to suggest they are similarly enslaved and powerless.

Questions

QUICK TEST
1. What different words and phrases are used to describe the rowing boat?
2. What makes the speaker feel powerful?
3. What makes the speaker feel powerless?
4. What could the mountain represent?

EXAM PRACTICE

Using one or two of the highlighted quotations to learn, write a paragraph exploring how Wordsworth presents the power of nature.

MY LAST DUCHESS by Robert Browning

Ferrara

That's my last Duchess painted on the wall,
Looking as if she were alive. I call
That piece a wonder, now: Frà Pandolf's hands
Worked busily a day, and there she stands.

5 Will't please you sit and look at her? I said
'Frà Pandolf' by design, for never read
Strangers like you that pictured countenance,
The depth and passion of its earnest glance,
But to myself they turned (since none puts by

10 The curtain I have drawn for you, but I)
And seemed as they would ask me, if they durst,
How such a glance came there; so, not the first
Are you to turn and ask thus. Sir, 'twas not
Her husband's presence only, called that spot

15 Of joy into the Duchess' cheek: perhaps
Frà Pandolf chanced to say 'Her mantle laps
Over my lady's wrist too much,' or 'Paint
Must never hope to reproduce the faint
Half-flush that dies along her throat': such stuff

20 Was courtesy, she thought, and cause enough
For calling up that spot of joy. She had
A heart – how shall I say? – too soon made glad,
Too easily impressed; she liked whate'er
She looked on, and her looks went everywhere.

25 Sir, 'twas all one! My favour at her breast,
The dropping of the daylight in the West,
The bough of cherries some officious fool
Broke in the orchard for her, the white mule

She rode with round the terrace – all and each

30 Would draw from her alike the approving speech,

Or blush, at least. She thanked men, – good! but thanked

Somehow – I know not how – as if she ranked

My gift of a nine-hundred-years-old name

With anybody's gift. Who'd stoop to blame

35 This sort of trifling? Even had you skill

In speech – (which I have not) – to make your will

Quite clear to such an one, and say, 'Just this

Or that in you disgusts me; here you miss,

Or there exceed the mark' – and if she let

40 Herself be lessoned so, nor plainly set

Her wits to yours, forsooth, and made excuse,

– E'en then would be some stooping; and I choose

Never to stoop. Oh sir, she smiled, no doubt,

Whene'er I passed her; but who passed without

45 Much the same smile? This grew; I gave commands;

Then all smiles stopped together. There she stands

As if alive. Will't please you rise? We'll meet

The company below, then. I repeat,

The Count your master's known munificence

50 Is ample warrant that no just pretence

Of mine for dowry will be disallowed;

Though his fair daughter's self, as I avowed

At starting, is my object. Nay, we'll go

Together down, sir. Notice Neptune, though,

55 Taming a sea-horse, thought a rarity,

Which Claus of Innsbruck cast in bronze for me!

This poem is about...

a 16th-century Italian duke, revealing a portrait of his dead wife; he is planning to marry again and, as he talks, it becomes apparent that he had his previous wife murdered.

How does the poet establish a sense of power at the start of the poem?

Browning uses nouns and proper nouns to establish the speaker's power. Referring to his 'Duchess' shows us he is a duke (traditionally the highest rank below the monarchy). His **nobility** is also shown in his language: he uses a high register, for example saying 'countenance' instead of face.

The Duke also refers to a painter, 'Frà Pandolf'. In the 16th century, only rich families could afford to have portraits of their family. The specific use of the artist's name implies that Frà Pandolf is also well-known, which suggests the Duke's wealth. When he says 'I call that piece a wonder', rather than talking about his feelings for his dead wife, it implies that he ranks the portrait's value above her memory.

Browning also presents power when the Duke points out on lines 9–10 that no one reveals the painting 'but I', with the statement confirming his status. The verb 'durst' (dare) on line 11 then indicates that people fear him. Notice also the amount of first person pronouns that are used (I, me, my, myself) to suggest his ego or high opinion of himself.

How do lines 13–24 introduce conflict and threat?

The Duke reveals his jealousy at the 'spot / Of joy' (repeated on line 21 to emphasise his annoyance) caused when the artist was polite to or flattered the Duchess. He dismissively refers to such words as 'stuff', indicating he never spoke to her with similar kindness. He says "twas not / Her husband's presence only", with the adverb 'only' suggesting he feels he should have been the only one she showed happiness towards.

Browning foreshadows our discovery of the truth about the Duchess's death when the Duke repeats the artist's description of her blushing: "the faint / Half-flush that dies along her throat".

The Duke's dislike of her happiness is developed on lines 21–24. A caesura, created by the second dash on line 22, emphasises the phrase 'too soon made glad' to show he felt she was too happy; the adverb 'too' is then repeated to highlight this idea. He feels she should only have given attention to him: 'her looks went everywhere'.

How are conflict and power explored further on lines 25–43?

The Duke was annoyed by how the Duchess took pleasure in small things, 'The bough of cherries [...] the white mule', not just his wealth and power. He felt this showed disrespect for his social position, 'as if she ranked / My gift of a nine-hundred-years-old name / With anybody's gift'; the noun phrase 'my gift' displays his arrogance (and reveals that she came from a lower status), while the verb 'ranked' indicates his obsession with **hierarchy**. He says her behaviour 'disgusts' him and the exclamation 'twas all one!' conveys his anger at her not valuing him above everything else.

The Duke's power is also patriarchal. He believes women are below men and should behave accordingly, using the abstract noun 'will' to show his wish to control. The verb 'lessoned' suggests women need teaching, and the verb phrases 'here you miss, / Or there exceed the mark' show they have a set role. He sees compromise on his part as demeaning, repeating the verb 'stooping'. The increased use of dashes also indicates the Duke's rising anger.

How does the mood of the poem get more menacing at the end?

Lines 45–46 describe the murder: 'This grew; I gave commands; / Then all smiles stopped together.' The short clauses create a blunt tone, portraying his lack of **remorse**. The noun 'commands' emphasises his power while the sibilance highlights his sinister distaste for her happiness. His attitude is also shown by calmly switching to his polite 'Will't please you rise?' on line 47.

In the final lines, the noun 'dowry' shows the Duke is arranging another marriage; it also suggests he is more interested in wealth and status than the girl. When he says 'his fair daughter's self [...] is my object', he appears to express his love but the noun 'object' implies that he just sees women as a **commodity**. This is emphasised when he boasts about his material wealth ('Which Claus of Innsbruck cast in bronze for me!'). The sculpture he refers to is symbolic of power as it features Neptune (a god, which the Duke also behaves as if he is) controlling a weaker species.

How does the poem's form contribute to the way meaning is conveyed?

The poem is a dramatic monologue. This allows the Duke to have power over his own story while removing power from the Duchess, who is only described by him.

The poem is written in rhyming couplets of iambic pentameter; this traditional use of metre and rhyme reflects the Duke's established family and position.

Additional context to consider

The poem is based on the fifth Duke of Ferrara (1533–1598), whose wife died mysteriously.

The Duke is talking to someone of a lower social status (an employee of the Count); he boasts about the murder, perhaps because his listener is powerless to do anything about it.

Like his 'last Duchess', his prospective wife will be socially inferior to him (as a Count was ranked lower than a Duke).

Browning was a **Victorian** poet; during this period, people became fascinated by new research in criminal psychology.

Poetic links

- Power in 'Ozymandias' or 'The Prelude'.
- Killing in 'Remains'.
- Status in 'The Émigrée'.
- The importance of honour in 'Kamikaze'.

Sample analysis

'My Last Duchess' and 'The Prelude' feature speakers who feel powerful. When Browning's Duke says 'Frà Pandolf's hands / Worked busily a day, and there she stands. / Will't please you sit and look at her?', he is showing off his wealth and position. Family portraits were a sign of status and the use of the proper noun implies the artist is celebrated; the adverb 'busily' could also suggest the Duke felt respected or feared by the artist. The offer to his listener shows he has power as the host and 'sit' also symbolises how the Duke is above the guest; that this line introduces his murderous boast also suggests he feels more powerful than – and untouchable by – his guest.

Wordsworth's lines, 'And, as I rose upon the stroke, my boat / Went heaving through the water like a swan', convey a similar feeling of power. The verbs 'rose' and 'heaving' suggest strength and dominance, while the simile shows pride in his power. Like 'My Last Duchess', the poem is written in iambic pentameter and this controlled rhythm could reflect the confident power of the two speakers.

Questions

QUICK TEST
1. How does Browning show the Duke boasting about his status?
2. How does Browning foreshadow the murder of the Duchess?
3. What words or phrases imply the Duke sees himself as above other people?
4. In what way is the statue of Neptune symbolic?

EXAM PRACTICE
Using one or two of the highlighted quotations to learn, write a paragraph exploring how Browning presents the speaker's sense of status.

THE CHARGE OF THE LIGHT BRIGADE by Alfred Tennyson

1. Half a league, half a league,
   Half a league onward,
   All in the valley of Death
       Rode the six hundred.
   'Forward, the Light Brigade!
   Charge for the guns!' he said:
   Into the valley of Death
       Rode the six hundred.

2. 'Forward, the Light Brigade!'
   Was there a man dismay'd?
   Not tho' the soldier knew
       Some one had blunder'd:
   Theirs not to make reply,
   Theirs not to reason why,
   Theirs but to do and die:
   Into the valley of Death
       Rode the six hundred.

3. Cannon to right of them,
   Cannon to left of them,
   Cannon in front of them
       Volley'd and thunder'd;
   Storm'd at with shot and shell,
   Boldly they rode and well,
   Into the jaws of Death,
   Into the mouth of Hell
       Rode the six hundred.

4. Flash'd all their sabres bare,
   Flash'd as they turn'd in air
   Sabring the gunners there,
   Charging an army, while
       All the world wonder'd:
   Plunged in the battery-smoke
   Right thro' the line they broke;
   Cossack and Russian
   Reel'd from the sabre-stroke
       Shatter'd and sunder'd.
   Then they rode back, but not
       Not the six hundred.

5. Cannon to right of them,
   Cannon to left of them,
   Cannon behind them
       Volley'd and thunder'd;
   Storm'd at with shot and shell,
   While horse and hero fell,
   They that had fought so well
   Came thro' the jaws of Death
   Back from the mouth of Hell,
   All that was left of them,
       Left of six hundred.

6. When can their glory fade?
   O the wild charge they made!
       All the world wonder'd.
   Honour the charge they made!
   Honour the Light Brigade,
       Noble six hundred!

This poem is about...

an attack by British **light cavalry**, led by Lord Cardigan, against the Russian army in 1854 during the Crimean War; because of miscommunication, the cavalry were sent to fight against a force much bigger than they were expecting and had to retreat after suffering very high casualties.

How does the first stanza establish an image of conflict?

The opening sentence introduces the metaphor 'the valley of Death' to foreshadow the tragedy of the poem. The repetition of this image throughout the poem is used to emphasise that the men are doomed.

The tricolon that begins the poem creates a mood of confidence and urgency as the men ride into battle. This mood is highlighted by including direct speech from the cavalry's commander; the exclamation marks and the imperative verbs 'forward' and 'charge' show he is encouraging and rallying his men.

How do the second and third stanzas establish a problem and heighten the conflict?

The fourth line of stanza 2 uses the verb 'blundered' to show that a mistake has been made and the men are being sent into a battle they cannot win.

The tragedy of this situation is created through the juxtaposition of their commander's rallying cry with the men knowing there has been an error. This is increased by Tennyson's description of their dutiful obedience, using a tricolon and rhyme, 'Theirs not to make reply, / Theirs not to reason why, / Theirs but to do and die', to create sympathy in the reader. The adverb 'but' (meaning only) implies that the lives of these men are not valued enough by the people in charge of the war.

A further tricolon is used in 'Cannon...' to emphasise that the men are outgunned. Tennyson also uses 'to right [...] to left [...] in front' to show that they are almost surrounded. Verbs ('volley'd [...] thunder'd [...] storm'd') convey the power of the opposition's artillery in order to create a frightening atmosphere.

A range of structural and phonological techniques are used to link the words together in stanza 3 (tricolons, repetition, rhyme, sibilance) to create the sense that the attack by the opposition is continuous.

Tennyson also uses personification ('jaws of Death [...] mouth of Hell') to convey the horror of armed conflict and emphasise how the odds are against the Light Brigade.

How do stanzas 4 and 5 present bravery and conflict?

The repetition of the verb 'flash'd', to describe the light cavalry's swords, incorporates symbolism of light to imply the British are good or have God on their side.

'Sabring' is juxtaposed with 'gunners' to remind the reader that the cavalry are at a disadvantage. This suggestion of bravery is heightened by hyperbole where 'All the world wonder'd' at the cavalry's heroic fighting.

Verbs are further used to show bravery as the cavalry 'plunged' into battle and managed to overpower some of the opposition, "Right thro' the line they broke', shocking the Russians ('Reel'd') and leaving them in disarray ('Shatter'd and sunder'd').

Tennyson uses parallelism in the fifth stanza, repeating most of the third stanza but replacing the men's bravery with defeat as each 'horse and hero fell'.

Instead of dwelling on their retreat, Tennyson uses euphemism ('rode back', 'came thro'', 'back from') so the men don't sound any less brave. Both stanzas end with a reminder that many of them died.

What is the message of the final stanza?

Stanza 6 uses different sentence functions to praise and commemorate the valour of the Light Brigade. The first line is a rhetorical question, implying their 'glory' will last forever. The second line is exclamative, portraying their remarkable bravery. The last two sentences are imperatives, urging the reader to 'Honour the Light Brigade'.

How does the poem's form contribute to the way meaning is conveyed?

'The Charge of the Light Brigade' is a narrative poem, retelling a true story. Its six stanzas could link to the six hundred men in the cavalry, with each stanza honouring one hundred men. The lines are quite short (usually six beats), creating a visual representation of the cavalry charging through the valley.

The poem is often written in dactylic dimeter. This means two sets of three beats: one stressed beat followed by two unstressed beats. For example, CAnnon to RIGHT of them. This is to reflect the sound of hooves and the excitement of the charge.

Starting with a stressed beat could represent the cavalry's determination, while the two unstressed beats make the rhythm 'fall' to represent the gradual, tragic fall of the men.

The poem has quite a traditional, formal structure: most lines are end-stopped and of a similar length, the metre is fairly uniform and there are clear rhyming patterns. This reflects the subject of the poem (a regiment of the army) as well as being appropriate for the respect that Tennyson wishes to show the men.

However, the poem isn't fully uniform: the lines and stanzas vary in length, and the rhyme scheme and metre aren't consistent. This could reflect the gradual breakdown of the cavalry's organisation and strength, which is also shown through the altering of the refrain at the end of each stanza.

Additional context to consider

The poem describes a group of men in the third person rather than offering a more intimate, individual or first person viewpoint.

Tennyson wrote his poem about six weeks after the actual battle. He was the **poet laureate** so he was expected to write formal, **patriotic** poems for the nation.

The general public were impressed by the valour of the cavalry but there was widespread criticism of those commanding the army. The poem includes both of these viewpoints.

Poetic links

- The presentation of war in 'Exposure' or 'Bayonet Charge'.
- Loss of power in 'Ozymandias'.
- Commemorating the dead in 'Poppies'.
- Bravery/cowardice in 'Kamikaze'.

Sample analysis

'The Charge of the Light Brigade' and 'Ozymandias' both depict a loss of power. Tennyson describes how the cavalry are 'Storm'd at with shot and shell, / While horse and hero fell', using nouns that remind the reader that the brave, sword-wielding cavalry are at a disadvantage. The sibilance connects the words describing the enemy attack to suggest that the onslaught is constant. The verbs 'storm'd' and 'fell' show the power of the opposition and its effect on the British forces, with the idea of cause and effect also being emphasised by the rhyming couplet (shell/fell).

In 'Ozymandias', Shelley's description 'on the sand, / Half sunk, a shatter'd visage lies' shows the fall of an entire kingdom. Perhaps due to the poem referencing an ancient Egyptian pharaoh, rather than a recent tragedy, Shelley's tone is far less sympathetic towards a loss of power than Tennyson. The sand can be seen as a symbolic warning of how power can be precarious. Like Tennyson, Shelley uses sibilance to emphasise a loss of power by connecting the words that indicate defeat (the adjectives 'sunk' and 'shatter'd', and the verb 'lies').

Questions

QUICK TEST
1. How does Tennyson foreshadow the tragic events of the poem?
2. How do the early stanzas portray a sense of confidence and urgency?
3. What poetic features are used to show that the cavalry are at a disadvantage?
4. How does Tennyson want us to view the cavalry at the end of the poem?

EXAM PRACTICE
Using one or two of the highlighted quotations to learn, write a paragraph exploring how Tennyson presents bravery.

EXPOSURE by Wilfred Owen

Our brains ache, in the merciless iced east winds that knive us...
Wearied we keep awake because the night is silent...
Low, drooping flares confuse our memory of the salient...
Worried by silence, sentries whisper, curious, nervous,
5   But nothing happens.

Watching, we hear the mad gusts tugging on the wire,
Like twitching agonies of men among its brambles.
Northward, incessantly, the flickering gunnery rumbles,
Far off, like a dull rumour of some other war.
10   What are we doing here?

The poignant misery of dawn begins to grow...
We only know war lasts, rain soaks, and clouds sag stormy.
Dawn massing in the east her melancholy army
Attacks once more in ranks on shivering ranks of grey,
15   But nothing happens.

Sudden successive flights of bullets streak the silence.
Less deadly than the air that shudders black with snow,
With sidelong flowing flakes that flock, pause, and renew,
We watch them wandering up and down the wind's nonchalance,
20   But nothing happens.

Pale flakes with fingering stealth come feeling for our faces –
We cringe in holes, back on forgotten dreams, and stare, snow-dazed,
Deep into grassier ditches. So we drowse, sun-dozed,

Littered with blossoms trickling where the blackbird fusses.

25   – Is it that we are dying?

Slowly our ghosts drag home: glimpsing the sunk fires, glozed
With crusted dark-red jewels; crickets jingle there;
For hours the innocent mice rejoice: the house is theirs;
Shutters and doors, all closed: on us the doors are closed, –

30   We turn back to our dying.

Since we believe not otherwise can kind fires burn;
Now ever suns smile true on child, or field, or fruit.
For God's invincible spring our love is made afraid;
Therefore, not loath, we lie out here; therefore were born,

35   For love of God seems dying.

Tonight, His frost will fasten on this mud and us,
Shrivelling many hands, puckering foreheads crisp.
The burying-party, picks and shovels in their shaking grasp,
Pause over half-known faces. All their eyes are ice,

40   But nothing happens.

This poem is about...

the terrible conditions in the First World War trenches as the soldiers wait for battle.

How do the first two stanzas present the soldiers' lives during the conflict?

Owen focuses on the terrible conditions with personification describing the power of the elements, 'merciless iced east winds that knive us'. The sibilance adds to the impression that the weather is attacking them and this technique is used throughout the poem.

Owen also conveys the sounds of conflict. The wind on the barbed wire is described using the disturbing simile 'Like twitching agonies of men', while onomatopoeia captures the sound of artillery ('rumbles'). The adverb 'incessantly' shows that the gunfire is a constant background noise and the soldiers' despair at their situation is conveyed in the rhetorical question that ends the second stanza, 'What are we doing here?'

Owen links the conditions to the soldiers' physical and emotional exhaustion, beginning with the phrase 'Our brains ache' and using the adjectives 'wearied [...] worried [...] curious, nervous'.

They are constantly waiting and the verbs 'whisper [...] watching [...] hear' suggest they are always alert to danger. This is emphasised by the idea that they 'keep awake because the night is silent'. The first three lines end with ellipses to convey this sense of continual restlessness. The constant waiting is summarised at the end of the first stanza (and repeated for emphasis in stanzas 3, 4 and 8): 'But nothing happens'.

How do stanzas 3 and 4 develop the mood of despair?

Dawn, usually a symbol of hope and new beginnings, is linked to 'poignant misery' to suggest there is no hope. Owen emphasises this through a tricolon of bleak images: 'We only know war lasts, rain soaks, and clouds sag stormy'.

The weather is personified as an attacking enemy army, 'Dawn massing in the east her melancholy army / Attacks once more in ranks on shivering ranks of grey'. Owen is suggesting that the freezing rain is even worse than the actual enemy because it is continual.

This idea is highlighted by the description of gunfire. Although the line 'Sudden successive flights of bullets streak the silence' is made frightening by the way the sibilance emphasises the sense of speed and sound, Owen describes the bullets as 'Less deadly than the air that shudders black with snow'. Using traditional colour symbolism, he replaces the typical beauty and purity of snow with death and evil. Alliteration and a tricolon then emphasise the unrelenting weather, 'flowing flakes that flock, pause, and renew'.

How do stanzas 5 and 6 present the conditions as killing the men?

The snow is personified, 'Pale flakes with fingering stealth come feeling for our faces', as if it is trying to freeze the men to death. Again, alliteration emphasises that this is continual. The men seem lowly or abased, almost like animals: 'We cringe in holes'. Their lack of hope is shown in the phrase 'forgotten dreams' and the rhetorical question 'Is it that we are dying?'

The 'ghosts' metaphor presents the soldiers as doomed. When they think of their homes (with an image of how much they'd value a warm fire, 'the sunk fires, glozed / With crusted dark-red jewels'), the doors are repeatedly 'closed' to symbolise that the soldiers will not survive the war. With the line 'We turn back to our dying', they seem to accept they will never return to England.

What is the message of the final two stanzas?

Stanza 7 shows the men are fighting for a cause: 'we believe not otherwise can kind fires burn; / Now ever suns smile true on child, or field, or fruit'. Similar techniques (personification, a tricolon) are used elsewhere in the poem but, here, they are much more hopeful for the future. However, the soldiers question the likelihood of this future and the belief that God is on their side: 'For love of God seems dying'. They see God as sending the weather that is killing them: 'His frost will fasten on this mud and us'.

The final image is of a 'burying-party'. The metaphor 'all their eyes are ice' depicts the soldiers' deaths from hypothermia; this could also be interpreted as the eyes of the men collecting the dead, suggesting they will suffer the same fate or have got so used to death they feel no emotion.

How does the poem's form contribute to the way meaning is conveyed?

This is an autobiographical poem. Regular rhyme and rhythm are used to reflect the continually bad conditions and the feeling that the war will never end. However, these structures are often disrupted to mirror the soldiers' tense and restless minds and the idea that they are broken and dying.

For example, the rhyme scheme is *abba* but often Owen only uses half-rhymes ('silent'/'salient'). Similarly, the metre is generally iambic hexameter but some lines (such as line 1) contain an extra stressed or unstressed beat that unsettles the rhythm. The fifth line of each stanza is also much shorter, interrupting the rhythm to emphasise Owen's repeated references to despair and death.

Additional context to consider

The poet, Wilfred Owen, fought and died in the First World War. Throughout the poem, he uses plural pronouns (we, our, us) to show he is speaking for all the soldiers that he fought alongside.

People at home didn't know about the terrible conditions so the title refers to the brutal conditions as well as to how Owen is exposing the truth.

Poetic links

- War in 'The Charge of the Light Brigade', 'Bayonet Charge' or 'Poppies'.
- The individual soldier in 'Bayonet Charge', 'Remains' or 'Kamikaze'.
- Conflict and suffering in 'War Photographer'.
- The power of nature in 'Storm on the Island' or 'The Prelude'.
- The transience of life in 'Ozymandias' or 'Tissue'.

Sample analysis

'Exposure' and 'The Charge of the Light Brigade' both present the horrors of war. Owen focuses on the brutal conditions, 'the merciless iced east winds that knive us', using personification to suggest that the men feel under attack by the weather. The verb 'knive' conveys their physical pain while the adjective 'merciless' show the men feel there is no respite, an idea emphasised by the use of sibilance and half-rhyme to build up the sense of a constant attack.

Tennyson focuses more on the fighting, perhaps because he wanted to celebrate the bravery of the Light Brigade. His use of anaphora in 'Cannon to right of them, / Cannon to left of them, / Cannon behind them' creates a similar image of soldiers being under constant attack. However, the dactylic dimeter creates a more exciting tone than in 'Exposure' where the iambic rhythm emphasises the sense of despair at the war never ending. Owen's language is also more graphic that Tennyson's, possibly due to his poem being autobiographical and him wanting to expose the reality of war.

Questions

QUICK TEST
1. How is the weather presented in the poem?
2. What technique is often used to convey the harshness of the weather?
3. What different senses are used to add realism to the poem?
4. In what way are the soldiers presented as without hope?

EXAM PRACTICE
Using one or two of the highlighted quotations to learn, write a paragraph exploring how Owen presents the brutal conditions of war.

STORM ON THE ISLAND by
Seamus Heaney

We are prepared: we build our houses squat,
Sink walls in rock and roof them with good slate.
This wizened earth has never troubled us
With hay, so, as you see, there are no stacks
5 Or stooks that can be lost. Nor are there trees
Which might prove company when it blows full
Blast: you know what I mean – leaves and branches
Can raise a tragic chorus in a gale
So that you can listen to the thing you fear
10 Forgetting that it pummels your house too.
But there are no trees, no natural shelter.
You might think that the sea is company,
Exploding comfortably down on the cliffs
But no: when it begins, the flung spray hits
15 The very windows, spits like a tame cat
Turned savage. We just sit tight while wind dives
And strafes invisibly. Space is a salvo,
We are bombarded by the empty air.
Strange, it is a huge nothing that we fear.

This poem is about...

the power of nature, depicted through the experiences of a small island community.

How do the first five lines set the scene?

The speaker opens the poem with a mood of confidence: 'We are prepared'. The choice of adjective makes it sound like the island community are about to face a difficult ordeal when the storm hits but that they will get through it. The plural pronoun ('we') suggests strength through unity.

Their preparations are long-term (conveyed through the verbs 'build [...] sink [...] roof'), suggesting that these storms are a regular occurrence. Images of strength and solidity show the community's determination as well as the power of the elements that they need to withstand: 'squat [...] walls [...] rock [...] slate'.

The island is presented as barren ('wizened earth') due to the harsh conditions but the speaker makes a joke about this, 'has never troubled us / With hay', to show how they are used to the conditions. The speaker also plays down the effects of the storm by displaying a positive attitude when commenting that the lack of hay means nothing can be lost in the gales.

How do lines 5–10 display a different attitude towards the storms?

The speaker makes the elements sound more frightening by describing how the wind 'blows full / Blast'. The alliterated plosives reflect the power of the storm while the enjambment extends the description onto the next line to imply that the gales last a long time. Despite the sense of confidence and community at the start of the poem, line 6 includes the speaker's wish for 'company', suggesting that the storm is intimidating.

A metaphor, 'tragic chorus', is used to describe the disturbing sound of wind in trees. However, there are no trees on the island and this is a sound the speaker actually *wants* to hear, explaining the benefit of being able to 'listen to the thing you fear / Forgetting that it pummels your house too'. The power of the storm is shown through the aggressive verb 'pummels' and the personification suggests it is so strong it is almost like a physical entity attacking the island. The verb 'fear' (repeated at the very end of the poem) makes it clear that the community is scared by these forces of nature.

The poet has the speaker address the reader directly, using the second person 'you' and a conversational tone. This encourages us to imagine, or empathise with, the experience of the island community during the storm.

How do lines 11–16 convey the power of the storm?

Line 11 creates a mood of danger and helplessness. The repetition of 'no' emphasises the absence of safety and this is also shown in the blunt and **unequivocal** tone implied by the short sentence.

The speaker describes the ocean crashing against the island as 'Exploding comfortably'. The contradictory verb and adverb form an oxymoron to imply the waves are insubstantial when compared to the power of the storm. Once the storm begins, the spray of the waves is 'flung' right across the island. A sense of awe at the power of the storm is shown in the description of how the water 'hits / The very windows'. A simile, 'spits like a tame cat / Turned savage', emphasises the almost crazed violence of the elements.

How do the last four lines emphasise the power of the storm?

Metaphor compares the wind to an attacking warplane, 'wind dives / And strafes', with the community presented as besieged victims, 'We just sit tight', hoping to survive. Warfare metaphors continue, depicting the wind as a 'salvo' (a simultaneous firing of artillery) and describing the frightened community as feeling 'bombarded'.

The speaker adds mystery to the power of the wind. The adverb 'invisibly' connects with the nouns 'space' and 'empty air' to suggest that the storm is beyond our understanding. This is summarised in the final line, 'Strange, it is a huge nothing that we fear', with the oxymoron ('huge nothing') conveying how the forces of nature are awesome and **unfathomable**.

How does the poem's form contribute to the way meaning is conveyed?

'Storm on the Island' is a dramatic monologue. It is written in blank verse; it doesn't rhyme but the nineteen lines are in iambic pentameter. The regular rhythm could reflect the constant attack of the storm while the lack of rhyme could represent the chaos and **discord** caused by the weather. Many of the lines also end with plosive sounds to evoke the harsh conditions.

Heaney breaks the rhythm at the start of line 7, using a spondee instead of an iamb so the opening two beats are both stressed: BLAST: YOU know WHAT i MEAN – leaves AND branCHES. This creates a more forceful introduction to the power of the elements.

The poem also features a lot of enjambment and caesuras so the poem doesn't always flow in the way the reader might expect, thereby mirroring the uncontrolled and unpredictable gusts of wind described in the poem.

Additional context to consider

The dramatic monologue and the repetition of the plural pronoun 'we' (used to describe the island community, rather than suggesting a link between the speaker and the reader) makes the reader an outsider.

Seamus Heaney's poetry is often rooted in a sense of place and explores our relationship with the landscape around us.

The lack of article ('A' or 'The') before the title suggests the poem is describing one of many storms. The location is not specifically named so it could relate to any island that experiences harsh weather conditions.

Poetic links

- The power of nature in 'The Prelude' or 'Exposure'.
- Places experiencing conflict in 'The Émigrée'.
- Powerlessness in 'London', 'The Prelude' or 'Exposure'.

Sample analysis

'Storm on the Island' and 'Exposure' both use figurative language to make the weather sound frightening. Heaney uses the simile 'spits like a tame cat / Turned savage' to describe how the storm affects the ocean. The verb suggests the violence of the elements while the contrasting adjectives show the extreme change caused by the weather. The enjambment emphasises how sudden and unpredictable this change can be.

After personifying the similarly unpredictable winds as 'mad gusts tugging on the wire', Owen also uses a simile to convey the terrifying sound caused by the wind. His description, 'Like twitching agonies of men among its brambles', links the weather to pain and slow death. The use of sound is particularly effective in immersing the reader in Owen's autobiographical poem as he attempts to convey the reality of conditions in the First World War.

Questions

QUICK TEST
1. What words and phrases are initially used to suggest the confidence of the island community?
2. What verb is repeated to show the speaker's true feelings about the storm?
3. What aggressive language is used to show the violence of the storm?
4. What recurring imagery is used to describe the power of the storm at the end of the poem?

EXAM PRACTICE
Using one or two of the highlighted quotations to learn, write a paragraph exploring how Heaney makes the weather sound frightening.

Suddenly he awoke and was running – raw
In raw-seamed hot khaki, his sweat heavy,
Stumbling across a field of clods towards a green hedge
That dazzled with rifle fire, hearing
5 Bullets smacking the belly out of the air –
He lugged a rifle numb as a smashed arm;
The patriotic tear that had brimmed in his eye
Sweating like molten iron from the centre of his chest, –

In bewilderment then he almost stopped –
10 In what cold clockwork of the stars and the nations
Was he the hand pointing that second? He was running
Like a man who has jumped up in the dark and runs
Listening between his footfalls for the reason
Of his still running, and his foot hung like
15 Statuary in mid-stride. Then the shot-slashed furrows

Threw up a yellow hare that rolled like a flame
And crawled in a threshing circle, its mouth wide
Open silent, its eyes standing out.
He plunged past with his bayonet toward the green hedge,
20 King, honour, human dignity, etcetera
Dropped like luxuries in a yelling alarm
To get out of that blue crackling air
His terror's touchy dynamite.

This poem is about...

a brief moment in a soldier's life; as he makes an assault on the enemy lines, we see how this experience affects him and shows different aspects of war.

How does the first stanza present conflict?

The poem begins *in medias res* (in the middle of things), 'Suddenly he awoke and was running', creating a suitably urgent mood. The adverb adds to this while the verb 'awoke' is meant metaphorically: his senses have quickly heightened.

There is a mood of nervousness, describing his 'sweat heavy' and repeating the adjective 'raw'. The latter could suggest the soldier isn't thinking about the situation, he is just behaving instinctively and 'running' towards the enemy. This is also shown when he is described as 'stumbling' towards 'a green hedge / That dazzled with rifle fire'. Referring to the 'hedge' instead of a specific enemy implies he is not considering what he's doing. This is emphasised by his lack of hesitation as he runs at the 'rifle fire' and the way the verb 'dazzled' suggests blindness.

The poet focuses on different senses. A metaphor conveys the sound of gunfire, 'Bullets smacking the belly out of the air', using alliteration and plosives to highlight the noise. A simile is used to describe the feel of the soldier's gun, 'a rifle numb as a smashed arm', with the adjective 'numb' again suggesting that he almost isn't aware of what he's doing. Both images contain violent language to build up the frightening atmosphere of war.

Describing the soldier's tear as 'patriotic' could refer to genuine patriotism or it could suggest he didn't want to admit his true fears before battle. It is turned into a disturbing simile, 'Sweating like molten iron', to suggest war is a terrifying, life-changing experience. The reference to the 'centre of his chest' could be describing his fears of being shot, or foreshadow his actual death.

How does the second stanza present the soldier differently?

A change comes across the soldier, 'In bewilderment then he almost stopped', as if he suddenly wonders what the point is of conflict.

A metaphor framed as a rhetorical question, 'In what cold clockwork of the stars and the nations / Was he the hand pointing that second?', shows the soldier's uncertainties. The 'clockwork' and 'stars' link to fate with the adjective 'cold' suggesting there is no sympathy in what is laid out for us. However, adding 'nations' could imply that politicians are controlling the fate of young men by sending them into battle to die. The image of 'the hand pointing that second' could suggest the soldier realises he has no control over his future; it is in the hands of others. A simpler interpretation of this metaphor could be that he wonders whether his time is up and he is about to be shot.

The soldier is now 'Listening between his footfalls for the reason / Of his still running', and the fact that no answer will come heightens the sense of his doubts. This is added to by the **surreal** simile in which the soldier seems to freeze in mid-air ('his foot hung like / Statuary in mid-stride'). The enjambment at the end of the stanza emphasises this strange stoppage of time.

How does the last stanza explore conflict further?

The poet focuses on a hare. Its movements look painful, 'rolled like a flame / And crawled in a threshing circle', with the 'circle' indicating it is trapped. This could symbolise the soldier who also cannot escape the war.

The similarity with the soldier is developed through 'its mouth wide / Open silent, its eyes standing out', suggesting innocence and terror. The notion that the soldier has been reduced to an animal continues in the line 'King, honour, human dignity, etcetera', with the dismissive 'etcetera' suggesting these values become valueless in battle. They are described using the noun 'luxuries' as if they cannot be afforded: it is a time simply for killing and survival.

The soldier resumes his attack, 'plunged past', and is now presented simply as a frightened weapon. 'Yelling alarm / To get out of that blue crackling air' captures his fear of the situation while the final line, 'His terror's touchy dynamite', shows how dangerous he is. His 'terror' is described as if it has taken control of him; the alliterated 't' resembles the ticking of a bomb about to go off and it is unclear whether the poem is leading towards his death or his killing of the enemy. The poem ends without resolution.

How does the poem's form contribute to the way meaning is conveyed?

This is a short narrative poem. Although arranged into three stanzas (each showing a different aspect of this moment in time), the poem is written in free verse: it doesn't rhyme and the lines differ in length with no fixed metre. This could be to reflect the sense of immediacy and terror as the soldier charges across the battlefield.

Enjambment adds to the speed and suddenness of the moment being described by not stopping the narrative at the end of each line. This can also be seen in the way the first 11 lines make up only one sentence.

Additional context to consider

Although the poem is placed in the past through the title's reference to a bayonet, the war, the soldier and the side he's on are not specified. This makes the poem more universal.

The poem is a psychological portrait, trying to imagine what is going through the soldiers mind, rather than a personal experience. Featuring just one soldier at one point in time focuses and intensifies the poem.

Poetic links

- War in 'Exposure', 'The Charge of the Light Brigade' or 'Poppies'.
- The individual soldier in 'Exposure', 'Remains' or 'Kamikaze'.
- Individuals' responses to conflict in 'Poppies', 'War Photographer' or 'Kamikaze'.

Sample analysis

'Bayonet Charge' and 'Kamikaze' explore soldiers' doubts in battle. Hughes's surreal simile, 'his foot hung like / Statuary in mid-stride', conveys a moment of uncertainty as the soldier runs at the enemy. The enjambment emphasises this mental pause where the soldier wonders what he is doing. The reference to statues links to memorials and the soldier's realisation that he might be running to his death; it could also relate to the notion that Hughes (considering the poem's lack of specific setting, time, etc.) is using this character to embody all soldiers and their doubts.

Garland also uses a simile to explore a soldier's doubts but the image is far less bleak. When he sees 'little fishing boats / strung out like bunting / on a green-blue translucent sea', the simple beauty of his life deters him from his suicide mission. The adjective 'translucent' could suggest the view provides a moment of clarity. The 'bunting' (symbolic of national celebration) is juxtaposed with humble 'fishing boats', to suggest the soldier realises he has to choose either patriotism and his country's politics or his family and individual happiness.

Questions

QUICK TEST
1. How does Hughes create a mood of urgency in the poem?
2. How does Hughes present the soldier's doubts?
3. How is the hare symbolic of the soldier?
4. What seems to be Hughes's final message about war?

EXAM PRACTICE
Using one or two of the highlighted quotations to learn, write a paragraph exploring how Hughes presents conflict as frightening.

On another occasion, we get sent out
to tackle looters raiding a bank.
And one of them legs it up the road,
probably armed, possibly not.

5   Well myself and somebody else and somebody else
are all of the same mind,
so all three of us open fire.
Three of a kind all letting fly, and I swear

I see every round as it rips through his life –
10   I see broad daylight on the other side.
So we've hit this looter a dozen times
and he's there on the ground, sort of inside out,

pain itself, the image of agony.
One of my mates goes by
15   and tosses his guts back into his body.
Then he's carted off in the back of a lorry.

End of story, except not really.
His blood-shadow stays on the street, and out on patrol
I walk right over it week after week.
20   Then I'm home on leave. But I blink

and he bursts again through the doors of the bank.
Sleep, and he's probably armed, possibly not.
Dream, and he's torn apart by a dozen rounds.
And the drink and the drugs won't flush him out –

25   he's here in my head when I close my eyes,
dug in behind enemy lines,
not left for dead in some distant, sun-stunned, sand-smothered land
or six-feet-under in desert sand,

but near to the knuckle, here and now,
30   his bloody life in my bloody hands.

This poem is about...

a soldier recounting how he shot a looter; at first he doesn't seem concerned but it becomes clear his actions haunt him.

How does the first stanza establish the situation?

The poem begins 'On another occasion', as if we are having a conversation with the speaker. The noun phrase suggests that what he is about to say is nothing out of the ordinary. The speaker's use of colloquial language ('we get sent out [...] one of them legs it') also makes this sound like an everyday event.

The speaker is a soldier, working as part of a peace-keeping force in another country: 'tackle looters raiding a bank'. The poet introduces a moral question of whether it is right to shoot the looter. When he is described as 'probably armed, possibly not', the adverbs show the soldiers may have a reason but that there is no definite justification.

How do stanzas 2–4 present the shooting?

The repetition of 'somebody else' could show the speaker protecting the identity of his colleagues. It could also link to the first stanza's suggestions that this wasn't unusual: he may have forgotten who he was with.

The speaker also repeats 'all' when describing the shooting. This could suggest he is not accepting sole blame or it could show they saw it as an enjoyable act of comradeship. This is emphasised by the reference to "Three of a kind' (perhaps an allusion to the heroic Three Musketeers) and the way the colloquial verb phrase for shooting, 'letting fly', has connotations of fun and freedom.

When the speaker says 'I swear' and vividly describes the shooting on lines 8 and 9, he sounds impressed with himself. The metaphor 'rips through his life' suggests his excitement, while 'broad daylight' uses traditional symbolism of light to indicate he thinks he has done something good. The soldiers' extreme behaviour is emphasised by 'a dozen times', although the speaker presents this as a kind of success. Their violent actions are an abuse of power and deliberately contrast with the role of peace-keeper established in the first stanza.

The speaker seems unconcerned by the killing when he describes the body as 'sort of inside out' but, as the sentence continues into the next stanza, the tone changes slightly and 'pain itself, the image of agony' could suggest more sympathy. However, this is overshadowed by the callous behaviour of one of his 'mates' who 'tosses his guts back into his body'. The verb choice shows a disregard for human life and this continues on line 16 when he's unceremoniously 'carted off'.

How do stanzas 5 and 6 develop the poem?

The short sentence on line 17 summarises their blunt indifference to the killing ('End of story') before introducing a different aspect ('except not really').

The metaphor 'blood-shadow' suggests the killing won't leave the speaker. The comment 'I walk right over it week after week' sounds like he is trying to ignore it but cannot. The reference to going 'home on leave' presents an escape but the caesura creates a dramatic pause that then highlights his inability to forget.

A tricolon – based around the verbs 'blink [...] sleep [...] dream' – emphasises that the killing constantly haunts him. He returns to the man's crime, the question of whether he was armed and his gruesome killing ('torn apart by a dozen rounds') as if trying, and failing, to justify the shooting. Line 24's metaphor 'flush him out' shows his wish to be free of the memory, with water linking to being cleansed of guilt. The reference to drinks and drugs shows he cannot cope with what he has done.

How do the final stanzas explore conflict?

The metaphor 'dug in behind enemy lines' shows the speaker feels attacked by the memory; it is almost real, 'near to the knuckle, here and now'. The poem's title is shown to be a double meaning: the remains of the looter and the killing remaining in the soldier's head.

When Armitage adds 'not left for dead in some distant, sun-stunned, sand-smothered land / or six-feet-under in desert sand', it implies the speaker wouldn't feel guilt if he was still in the war zone. The compound adjectives suggest it's possible to be blind to bad things and cover them up. This suggests conflict changes people: they do things and justify things they never would at home.

The speaker's shame is summarised in the final line, 'his bloody life in my bloody hands', using parallelism to highlight his abuse of power when he shot the looter and his current, inescapable feelings of guilt.

How does the poem's form contribute to the way meaning is conveyed?

The poem is a dramatic monologue. It is written in free verse and this, along with the use of enjambment, makes the poem read like realistic speech.

The poem is organised into quatrains. This clear construction contrasts with the irregular metre to reflect how the soldiers act outside of regulations, abusing the power of their position in a way that is not suitable for an army. The last stanza has only two lines, emphasising the final image of guilt and indicating that the speaker cannot continue.

Additional context to consider

The poem appears to draw on newspaper reports of alleged abuses of power by British soldiers during the Iraq War. As it's written like part of a conversation, the speaker remains unnamed and could represent any dishonourable soldier.

Armitage doesn't present a judgement on the speaker. Instead, the dramatic monologue provides the reader with the speaker's realistic and therefore personally biased viewpoint, encouraging us to make our own judgements.

Poetic links

- Killing in 'My Last Duchess'.
- The aftermath of war in 'Poppies'.
- Ethics during conflict in 'War Photographer'.

- How war affects individuals in 'Bayonet Charge' or 'War Photographer'.

Sample analysis

'Remains' and 'My Last Duchess' use dramatic monologues to present different attitudes to killing. Armitage's speaker is haunted by guilt. The line 'Dream, and he's torn apart by a dozen rounds' forms part of a tricolon that emphasises his constant thoughts about the killing of the looter. The verb 'dream' shows there's no escape, even when sleeping. The killing is retold from stanza 2 with the metaphor creating a more brutal, less celebratory version of the act.

In contrast, Browning's speaker feels no guilt. The poem's setting is linked more strongly to patriarchy and class privilege so when he describes how his wife 'ranked / My gift of a nine-hundred-years-old name / With anybody's gift', he appears to feel justified in having her killed. The noun phrase describing his social status suggests he considers himself superior to others, while the juxtaposition of the two possessive determiners shows he felt disrespected by his wife and believes it was she who was in the wrong.

Questions

QUICK TEST
1. What is the effect of the poem's colloquial language?
2. What words and phrases show the soldiers' disrespect for human life?
3. What structural technique emphasises the speaker's continual thoughts about the killing?
4. What metaphor shows he wants to rid himself of the guilt?

EXAM PRACTICE
Using one or two of the highlighted quotations to learn, write a paragraph exploring how Armitage presents abuses of power.

POPPIES by Jane Weir

Three days before Armistice
    Sunday

and poppies had already been
    placed

on individual war graves. Before
    you left,

I pinned one onto your lapel,
    crimped petals,

5   spasms of paper red, disrupting
    a blockade

of yellow bias binding around
    your blazer.

Sellotape bandaged around
    my hand,

I rounded up as many white cat
    hairs

as I could, smoothed down your
    shirt's

10 upturned collar, steeled the
    softening

of my face. I wanted to graze
    my nose

across the tip of your nose, play at

being Eskimos like we did when

you were little. I resisted the
    impulse

15 to run my fingers through the
    gelled

blackthorns of your hair. All my
    words

flattened, rolled, turned into felt,

slowly melting. I was brave,
    as I walked

with you, to the front door, threw

20 it open, the world overflowing

like a treasure chest. A split
    second

and you were away, intoxicated.

After you'd gone I went into your
    bedroom,

released a song bird from its cage.

25 Later a single dove flew from the
    pear tree,

and this is where it has led me,

skirting the church yard walls,
    my stomach busy

making tucks, darts, pleats,
    hat-less, without

a winter coat or reinforcements
    of scarf, gloves.

30 On reaching the top of the hill
    I traced

the inscriptions on the war
    memorial,

leaned against it like a wishbone.

The dove pulled freely against the
    sky,

an ornamental stitch. I listened,
    hoping to hear

35 your playground voice catching
    on the wind.

This poem is about...

a woman remembering her son who has died in a war; the focus is on people left at home rather than those who have gone to fight.

How does the first stanza set the scene?

The poem takes place at different points in time, not always making changes clear. This conveys how a powerful feeling is not singular but attached to other moments and emotions. The first time mentioned, 'Three days before Armistice Sunday', indicates the poem is linked to war but does not specify which war.

Time shifts to 'Before you left', describing the speaker pinning a poppy to her son's blazer. This symbol of remembrance commemorates the deaths of soldiers in the First World War and all subsequent wars. It is described as 'crimped petals, / spasms of paper red, disrupting a blockade / of yellow bias'. The metaphorical use of 'blockade' could link to a modern war while 'spasms of [...] red' could indicate the way her son died. Although this could be the day her son leaves for war, the reference to 'yellow bias binding around your blazer' suggests a new school uniform. This is an example of the poet deliberately **conflating** memories and thoughts.

The poppy's description introduces a recurring lexical field of needlework ('pinned [...] crimped [...] bias binding') to focus the poem on the mother. The speaker also never specifically mentions her son's death; it is something we infer from her words.

How does stanza 2 present the mother's feelings?

Her love is shown through her care for his appearance; the verb 'smoothed' sounds particularly gentle. Other word choices have deliberate double meanings: the verb phrase 'rounded up' could allude to his work as a soldier while the adjective 'bandaged' could link to his injuries.

The metaphor 'steeled the softening / of my face' juxtaposes two verbs with opposite meanings but joined by alliteration to convey her struggle to hide her feelings. 'Steeled' contains another allusion to war, suggesting the metal of a gun. Verbs further convey emotional struggle when 'I wanted' on line 11 is followed by 'I resisted' on line 14.

She wants to touch her son before he leaves and keep him innocent: 'graze my nose / across the tip of your nose [...] like we did when you were little [...] run my fingers through'. At the end of the stanza, a metaphor conveys her inability to find the right words to say; continuing the list across two stanzas delays its completion in order to reflect this struggle.

How do stanzas 3 and 4 develop the mother's feelings?

Her description of her bravery relates to keeping her emotions under control as well as her son's role as a soldier. When she 'threw' the door open, the verb reveals her attempt to seem confident. The subsequent simile, 'the world overflowing / like a treasure chest', could convey the strange beauty of the day she last saw her son or be another image of struggling to control her emotions and being unable to keep her precious son.

Her sadness at her last sight of him is emphasised through the shortness of the sentence. The adjective 'intoxicated' shows his excitement in contrast to her feelings of loss (then, and now that he's dead). The phrase 'After you'd gone' could similarly be after he's left or when he has died. The metaphor 'released a song bird from its cage' conveys her finally releasing her emotions.

'Later' provides another **ambiguous** shift in time. She is led by a dove (a symbol of peace) to the churchyard. Her grief is described metaphorically through a tricolon of needlework images ('my stomach busy / making tucks, darts, pleats'). There is a sense that she feels exposed, emotionally as well as physically, making another allusion to war in 'reinforcements'.

In the last stanza, running her fingers over 'the inscriptions on the war memorial', it is unclear whether her son has died at this point or whether she is just fearing for his life. There are similar multiple possibilities in the final image of her listening for her son's 'playground voice'. The 'wishbone' simile could suggest a hope to keep him safe or a wish that he is still alive; it could also imply that she feels at breaking point. The dove metaphor conveys her heightened feelings and perhaps a sense that, without her son, her life is unravelling.

How does the poem's form contribute to the way meaning is conveyed?

'Poppies' is a lyric poem addressing the speaker's (presumably dead) son; it can also be described as an elegy.

The poem is written in free verse and contains a lot of enjambment and caesuras. This lack of a fixed rhythm reflects how the poem is constructed around different memories merging into each other (rather than one clear moment), as well as the idea at the end that her life is unravelling.

Despite the free verse, the poem is divided into stanzas; however, these vary in length. This could represent the way, especially in the second and third stanzas, she tries to control her emotions.

Additional context to consider

The speaker is addressing her son, which makes the poem more intimate and moving. Also, things that they would know (the war he fought in, how he died, etc.) are left unspoken, which allows the poem to be more universal, not just about one specific parent and child.

The poet uses language to convey that this is a mother's point of view. A lot of everyday images are used to help the reader relate to the experience.

Poetic links

- The aftermath of war in 'Remains'.
- Attitudes to war at home in 'War Photographer'.
- Attitudes to sacrifice in 'Kamikaze'.
- The power of memory in 'The Émigrée'.

Sample analysis

'Poppies' and 'Remains' use metaphor to present the after-effects of war on individuals. Weir uses the image 'After you'd gone I went into your bedroom, / released a song bird from its cage' to convey her speaker's grief. The reference to a 'cage' shows how she has been trying to control her emotions. The familiar bedroom setting is also poignant, symbolising her impossible wish to have stopped her son growing up and to have kept him at home.

Armitage also uses metaphor, showing how his speaker is haunted by his war-time actions. The lines 'he's here in my head when I close my eyes, / dug in behind enemy lines' use a military image that matches the speaker's past. He appears to feel under attack by the memory of the looter that he shot. Both poets have used free verse, possibly reflecting how their speakers are struggling to control the emotions that they have been left with.

Questions

QUICK TEST
1. What recurring imagery is used that links to domesticity?
2. How might the poppy in stanza 1 link to her son's death?
3. Which words contain a double meaning that could link to war?
4. Which images suggest the speaker tries to control her emotions?

EXAM PRACTICE
Using one or two of the highlighted quotations to learn, write a paragraph exploring how Weir presents the speaker's feelings about her son.

WAR PHOTOGRAPHER
by Carol Ann Duffy

In his darkroom he is finally alone
with spools of suffering set out in ordered rows.
The only light is red and softly glows,
as though this were a church and he
5 a priest preparing to intone a Mass.
Belfast. Beirut. Phnom Penh. All flesh is grass.

He has a job to do. Solutions slop in trays
beneath his hands, which did not tremble then
though seem to now. Rural England. Home again
10 to ordinary pain which simple weather can dispel,
to fields which don't explode beneath the feet
of running children in a nightmare heat.

Something is happening. A stranger's features
faintly start to twist before his eyes,
15 a half-formed ghost. He remembers the cries
of this man's wife, how he sought approval
without words to do what someone must
and how the blood stained into foreign dust.

A hundred agonies in black-and-white
20 from which his editor will pick out five or six
for Sunday's supplement. The reader's eyeballs prick
with tears between the bath and pre-lunch beers.
From the aeroplane he stares impassively at where
he earns his living and they do not care.

This poem is about...

the nature of war photography; focusing on an imaginary war photographer, the poet explores the practice, its ethics and its impact.

How does stanza 1 present the work of a war photographer?

The opening sentence has a **sombre** tone: 'In the darkroom he is finally alone'. The adverb indicates eagerness to develop his photographs or could suggest his job is stressful and he needs solitude. The phrase 'spools of suffering set out in ordered rows' compares the camera film being developed to bodies in a mortuary. The sibilance continues the sombre tone while the noun phrase 'ordered rows' suggests he detaches himself from his distressing subject matter and works in a cold, methodical way.

The darkroom is compared to a church, conveying how seriously he takes his work. The red light symbolises the blood of battlefields. However, the adverb 'softly' implies his safety and comfort, compared to the people left behind. 'Mass' is linked to Christ's sacrifice; this could be the photographer thinking about people he has seen die or could suggest he sees himself as making personal sacrifices to document wars.

The tricolon 'Belfast. Beirut. Phnom Penh' focuses on different civil wars. Each proper noun is a single sentence, creating respectful pauses that emphasise the significance of each place. The phrase 'All flesh is grass' is from the Bible and means that life doesn't last; it is often used as an **epitaph** to honour the dead, suggesting the photographer's respect for the victims of war.

How does stanza 2 explore the photographer's feelings about his work?

Linking back to line 2, the short sentence 'He has a job to do' suggests the photographer is professional and dispassionate. However, he seems to be reminding himself of this in order to focus on his work. The description, 'his hands, which did not tremble then / though seem to now', implies that, away from a warzone, he struggles not to dwell on the **atrocities** he has witnessed.

Like line 3, the short sentence 'Rural England' suggests the comparative ease and comfort of his life. He seems aware of this in the phrase 'ordinary pain which simple weather can dispel'. He perhaps feels guilt for the way he makes his living or for the people he leaves behind, comparing England's fields to minefields in a warzone. The final line, 'running children in a nightmare heat', is a specific allusion to a famous war photograph of a child running from a napalm attack in Vietnam.

How does stanza 3 explore the photographer's feelings further?

The short sentence, 'Something is happening', describes the photographs being developed and how the photographer is affected by his memories.

The photograph is described as if it is alive, 'features / faintly start to twist', with the verb linking to the pain of the dead man. The metaphor 'half-formed ghost' refers to the man's death and the photograph not being fully developed yet. Although gruesome, it implies these photographs are important to show the reality of war. This is highlighted by the imperative verb 'must', despite photographing someone's death seeming inappropriate and insensitive.

The description of how the 'blood stained' suggests these countries will not fully recover from their wars and neither will he ('He remembers the cries').

How does the last stanza explore other attitudes to war photography?

The powerful metaphor, 'A hundred agonies in black-and-white', describes the atrocities the photographer has documented. But this is undermined by the attitude of the newspaper editor: the verb phrase 'pick out' shows the photographs are judged for their impact on readers; the noun 'supplement' implies the photographs have no individual importance and are just add-ons. The description of the newspaper reader suggests the photographs have only a temporary impact and we have become **desensitised** to images of war, emphasised by the internal rhyme of 'tears' and 'beers'.

The final sentence returns to the unique nature of war photography. The adverb 'impassively' repeats his lack of emotion but it has been suggested this is to keep him focused; however, the reference to 'earns his living' reminds us he also makes money from war. The phrase 'they do not care' implies he knows his photographs have no lasting impact, yet he keeps working. Deliberately, the subject is not concluded by the poet; we are left to form our own opinions.

How does the poem's form contribute to the way meaning is conveyed?

The poem is arranged in four sestets, many of the lines are written in iambic pentameter and there is a repeated *abbcdd* rhyme scheme. This reflects the controlled, methodical approach that the war photographer takes to his work.

However, not all lines follow the same metre and the rhythm is disrupted further through enjambment and caesura. This could mirror how, once at home, the war photographer's feelings break through his detached exterior. It could also represent how war photography is not clear-cut and simple to define, having historical importance but raising complex ethical questions.

Additional context to consider

The third person perspective creates a portrait of the war photographer; we don't get his own voice but neither does the poet judge him. This detached view encourages readers to make up their own minds.

Details are included that British readers can relate to (such as Belfast, fields, Sunday supplement, bath, beer) so they can put themselves into the context of the poem and consider their own responses to images of war in the media.

Poetic links

- How war affects individuals in 'Bayonet Charge' or 'Remains'.
- Ethics during conflict in 'Remains'.

- Attitudes to war at home in 'Poppies'.
- Conflict and suffering in 'Exposure'.

Sample analysis

'War Photographer' and 'Bayonet Charge' explore how war affects individuals. In Duffy's poem, the man photographs a dead body in a way that would normally seem inappropriate. The lines 'he sought approval / without words to do what someone must' use a modal verb to show he feels he has no choice because of the situation he is in. Although it specifies he gets permission, it is clear he places documenting war above more usual emotions and reactions to death. There is a sense that he is sacrificing normal values for a greater purpose.

A similar change comes over Hughes's soldier. The simile 'King, honour, human dignity, etcetera / Dropped like luxuries in a yelling alarm' suggests that, in the context of battle, normal values do not apply. Ending the list with 'etcetera' is particularly dismissive, while the noun 'luxuries' implies that war simply becomes about survival. This is emphasised by the noun phrase 'yelling alarm' as the soldier transforms into more of a weapon than a human being.

Questions

QUICK TEST
1. What is the effect of the opening sentence?
2. What words and phrases suggest the comfort in which the photographer lives?
3. Which word in stanza 3 suggests he sees his job as necessary?
4. What is suggested about the impact of his photographs?
EXAM PRACTICE
Using one or two of the highlighted quotations to learn, write a paragraph exploring how Duffy presents conflict and suffering.

Paper that lets the light
shine through, this
is what could alter things.
Paper thinned by age or touching,

5   the kind you find in well-used
      books,
    the back of the Koran, where
      a hand
    has written in the names and
      histories,
    who was born to whom,

    the height and weight, who
10   died where and how, on which
      sepia date,
    pages smoothed and stroked and
      turned
    transparent with attention.

    If buildings were paper, I might
    feel their drift, see how easily
15   they fall away on a sigh, a shift
    in the direction of the wind.

    Maps too. The sun shines through
    their borderlines, the marks
    that rivers make, roads,

20   railtracks, mountainfolds,
    Fine slips from grocery shops
    that say how much was sold
    and what was paid by credit card
    might fly our lives like paper kites.

25   An architect could use all this,
    place layer over layer, luminous
    script over numbers over line,
    and never wish to build again
      with brick

    or block, but let the daylight break
30   through capitals and monoliths,
    through the shapes that pride
      can make,
    find a way to trace a grand design

    with living tissue, raise a structure
    never meant to last,
35   of paper smoothed and stroked
    and thinned to be transparent,

    turned into your skin.

This poem is about...

how the delicacy of tissue paper represents the fragility of human life; the poet suggests that, if the world was made of paper, we would all see this fragility and take more care.

How do the first three stanzas describe tissue paper?

Tissue paper is used throughout the poem as an extended metaphor for life.

Using traditional symbolism, 'lets the light / shine through', the opening sentence presents tissue paper as a source of hope and goodness. Enjambment is used to emphasise this image of optimism, extending it across two lines to represent hope and goodness spreading.

The qualities of paper are linked to universal values that we share as a people. It is related to experience ('age or touching'), faith ('the Koran'), history ('the names and histories'), family ('who was born to whom') and remembrance ('who / died where and how'). The list builds up the importance of these values, suggesting that, in our modern society filled with conflict, they are too often forgotten. The final tricolon, 'smoothed and stroked and turned / transparent with attention', uses verbs linked to gentleness to suggest the world is delicate and needs more tenderness: we should treat it like it's made of tissue paper.

How do stanzas 4–6 use the tissue paper metaphor?

Stanza 4 imagines buildings made of tissue paper: 'I might / feel their drift, see how easily / they fall away on a sigh'. The poet suggests the ease with which we destroy cities and historic buildings in wars; if they looked more delicate, perhaps we would take more care of them. The noun 'shift' could be recommending a change to the way we see the world.

Stanza 5 imagines maps being made of tissue paper. The poet lists features of maps that distinguish one nation from another, 'borderlines, the marks / that rivers make, roads, / railtracks, mountainfolds', suggesting that we seek to separate ourselves from other countries. The verb phrase 'sun shines through' returns to light as a symbol of hope, creating an image of these divisions being erased.

The sixth stanza imagines the light pouring through tissue paper versions of receipts, 'how much was sold / and what was paid by credit card'. This image of **capitalism** being erased is linked to freedom. The simile, 'might fly our lives like paper kites', features another modal verb (like line 3) to suggest something to aspire to. The extended metaphor of tissue paper suggests we need to see through the things that hold us back from happiness.

How do the last four stanzas present the poem's message?

Line 25, 'An architect could use all this', refers back to the different ideas presented so far about seeing the world in a different way. The seventh stanza then starts to describe the rebuilding of the world as a gentler place, 'layer over layer, luminous [...] never wish to build again with brick / or block', continuing the symbolic use of light and contrasting soft lateral l sounds with harsh plosive b sounds.

The poem describes 'capitals and monoliths, / [...] the shapes that pride can make', using cities to represent the worst of humankind. They are presented as places of sin and arrogance ('pride'), linked to capitalism and politics ('capitals'), and filled with **power structures** that resist change ('monoliths'). However, enjambment is used to emphasise how the symbolic light can 'break / through' these places and lead to a better vision of the future, 'a grand design'.

At this point in the poem the extended metaphor of tissue paper changes to 'living tissue', emphasising the idea that the world needs to be built around an awareness of the fragility of life.

The image of building 'a structure / never meant to last' focuses on the **transience** of life and argues against the way humankind focuses too much on competition and one nation appearing stronger than another. The final lines of the ninth stanza echo the tricolon from stanza 3 to reiterate the importance of a world that is looked after and is 'transparent' (based on honesty and truth).

The last line is given its own stanza to highlight the importance of its message. The metaphor 'turned into your skin' can, like much of the poem, be interpreted in different ways. It may suggest that we need to become citizens of the world rather than disparate individuals, or it could describe treating the world as if it is our own skin, or building a world that reflects the best, gentlest attributes of the human race.

How does the poem's form contribute to the way meaning is conveyed?

The poem is organised into ten stanzas: nine quatrains and a single, final line. The stanzas could represent the different layers of paper that are described throughout the poem and are imagined being used to rebuild the world.

The lines are written in free verse, perhaps representing the airy lightness of tissue paper. This reflects the poem's criticism of social and political structures, and the contrasting focus on freedom.

Additional context to consider

Imtiaz Dharker was born in Pakistan and brought up in Scotland. The poem blends allusions to Asia (Koran, mountainfolds), the West (grocery shops, credit cards) and things that bridge the two (kites, capitals).

The repeated focus on paper and light, recognisable all around the world, emphasises the global nature of this poem.

Poetic links

- The transience of life in 'Ozymandias' or 'Exposure'.
- The wish to remove power structures in 'London'.
- Imagining places free from conflict in 'The Émigrée'.
- Contrasting peace in 'Tissue' with war in 'The Charge of the Light Brigade', 'Exposure', 'Bayonet Charge' or 'War Photographer'.

Sample analysis

'Tissue' and 'War Photographer' present contrasting images of peace and war. Dharker's extended tissue metaphor imagines a place 'of paper smoothed and stroked / and thinned to be transparent' to convey a more peaceful world that values the fragility of human life. The tricolon of verbs focuses on delicacy and gentleness, emphasised by the long vowel sounds in the first line. The noun transparent also suggests the role that truth and openness play in peace.

In contrast, Duffy's poem presents a world of constant war and death. The line 'Belfast. Beirut. Phnom Penh. All flesh is grass' shows the world as it is, rather than Dharker's view of how it 'could' be. The capital cities are linked to civil war and Duffy emphasises them through short sentences; she also uses sound, like Dharker, and implies conflict through plosives. The fragility of human life also appears in this poem, through the biblical allusion, but it features as an epitaph rather than a point of optimism.

Questions

QUICK TEST
1. What technique is used throughout the poem to link ideas to tissue paper?
2. What modal verbs are used to show the poem offering possible change?
3. What human values are linked to paper in stanzas 2 and 3?
4. What words and phrases suggest a criticism of modern society?

EXAM PRACTICE
Using one or two of the highlighted quotations to learn, write a paragraph exploring how Dharker presents a wish to remove power structures.

THE ÉMIGRÉE by Carol Rumens

There once was a country... I left it as a child
but my memory of it is sunlight-clear
for it seems I never saw it in that November
which, I am told, comes to the mildest city.
5   The worst news I receive of it cannot break
my original view, the bright, filled paperweight.
It may be at war, it may be sick with tyrants,
but I am branded by an impression of sunlight.

The white streets of that city, the graceful slopes
10   glow even clearer as time rolls its tanks
and the frontiers rise between us, close like waves.
That child's vocabulary I carried here
like a hollow doll, opens and spills a grammar.
Soon I shall have every coloured molecule of it.
15   It may by now be a lie, banned by the state
but I can't get it off my tongue. It tastes of sunlight.

I have no passport, there's no way back at all
but my city comes to me in its own white plane.
It lies down in front of me, docile as paper;
20   I comb its hair and love its shining eyes.
My city takes me dancing through the city
of walls. They accuse me of absence, they circle me.
They accuse me of being dark in their free city.
My city hides behind me. They mutter death,
25   and my shadow falls as evidence of sunlight.

This poem is about...

a displaced woman, thinking about the country she left; her thoughts are nostalgic but admit how the country has changed for the worse.

How does the first stanza establish an impression of her homeland?

An émigrée is a female emigrant: someone who has left their country, often in political **exile**. The title implies the speaker's homeland is run by a powerful tyrannical regime. The opening line sounds like a fairytale, 'There was once a country...', suggesting her memories seem almost unbelievable today. The ellipsis represents the speaker taking us back in time.

In the description, 'my memory of it is sunlight-clear', the compound adjective introduces a sense of beauty and truth. However, 'sunlight' suggests she is only remembering the good things; this sense of an unreliable narrator links to her admission that she 'left it as a child'. The metaphor, 'bright, filled paperweight', implies an idealised impression of happiness and safety.

Her reference to 'that November' indicates a historical event that changed things while drawing on the seasons to symbolise a time of unhappiness and dying. She admits she has heard the 'worst news' about the place and says it 'may be at war, it may be sick with tyrants'. The repeated modal verb suggests she does not want to believe the truth while the personification creates a powerful image of a dictatorship.

How does the second stanza explore the changes to her homeland?

Traditional symbols of purity and goodness appear in 'The white streets of that city, the graceful slopes / glow'. To show reality cannot be ignored, the same sentence features a more troubled image: 'time rolls its tanks / and the frontiers rise between us, close like waves'. Personification again conveys a powerful regime while the simile shows she feels cut off from her homeland.

The speaker contrasts a simile about her limited childhood view ('like a hollow doll') with a metaphor that implies she has elaborated on her memories ('opens and spills a grammar'). This repeats the idea of her unreliable narration and when she says 'Soon I shall have every coloured molecule of it', the metaphor implies she constructs this **idealised** view for her own benefit. She needs to remember her homeland happily because it brings her pleasure and gives her hope for its future: 'It tastes of sunlight'.

However, she admits 'It may by now be a lie, banned by the state'. The abstract noun 'lie' suggests her version of the country no longer exists. It could also imply the current regime is so powerful it has rewritten history, making her memory untrue. The verb 'banned' conveys the **oppressive** power of the regime, indicating that even her old language has been prohibited.

How does the last stanza present the speaker's feelings?

Like line 11, the stanza opens with a sense that she is cut off from her homeland. The metaphor 'I have no passport' is followed by the more direct 'there's no way back at all'. The speaker then presents the power of her memories by describing the city as if it travels to her, 'in its own white plane'.

Rather than present her homeland in turmoil, she uses figurative language to compare it to a calm pet and includes gentle verbs and adjectives: 'lies down in front of me, docile as paper'. Her love of the city is captured in the line 'I comb its hair and love its shining eyes', although the verb 'comb' also links to her deliberate idealism.

Personification shows how the memory brings her happiness: 'My city takes me dancing'. However, the poem ends with the understanding that she wouldn't be welcome in her homeland. The sudden and repeated use of the plural pronoun 'they' presents the regime (and possibly how they have manipulated the minds of the population against emigrants like her) and creates a threatening mood. This is emphasised by the verbs 'accuse' and 'circle', and the way in which 'They mutter death'.

Adjectives are used ironically, 'They accuse me of being dark in their free city', to show how tyrannical regimes actually present themselves as forces for good. Oppression is shown through personification, 'My city hides behind me', but the poem ends with a final symbolic image of hope for a better future: 'my shadow falls as evidence of sunlight'.

How does the poem's form contribute to the way meaning is conveyed?

'The Émigrée' is a dramatic monologue. It is arranged into two octaves and a nonet; the additional line in the final stanza could mirror the hopeful view that life goes on and a better future is possible. This view is supported by the way each stanza ends with the optimistic symbol of 'sunlight'.

The poem is written in free verse, perhaps mirroring the mood of freedom that she applies to her memories of her homeland. This could contrast with a sense of poetic restriction (created by dividing the poem into stanzas and using lines of a similar length that are increasingly end-stopped) to represent the conflict between her idealised memories and the oppressive nature of the current regime.

Additional context to consider

The dramatic monologue doesn't specify a name, time or country, allowing the reader to imagine the voice of any emigrant.

Because the memory of the homeland is from a child's perspective, the descriptions are often more simple and childlike compared to those about the country under its current regime.

Poetic links

- The power of memory in 'Poppies'.
- Places experiencing conflict in 'Storm on the Island'.
- Imagining places free from conflict in 'Tissue'.
- The power to make others outsiders in 'Checking Out Me History'.

Sample analysis

'The Émigrée' and 'Tissue' present visions of places free from conflict. Rumens's poem features an emigrant's memory of her homeland, 'The white streets of that city, the graceful slopes / glow', using symbols of purity ('white') and goodness ('glow') to present an idealised view. The gentleness of the last three words, emphasised by the long vowels, suggests a place without restriction. It is made clear the memory was formed in childhood, linking to the poet's use of simple, happy images.

Dharker's use of language is more complex, using the extended metaphor of tissue paper to present a world free from cruelty and war. The opening description, 'Paper that lets the light / shine through', uses similar symbolism to Rumens, with enjambment making the line run on to represent the idea of goodness spreading. The verb 'lets' implies liberty and Dharker creates a transparent, delicate world that therefore values truth and gentleness. Both poets write in free verse, avoiding traditional poetic structures, to reflect their visions of freedom.

Questions

QUICK TEST
1. When was the impression of the speaker's homeland formed?
2. What words and phrases in stanza 2 suggest a violent regime taking over?
3. What is meant by 'I have no passport'?
4. What is significant about the end of each stanza?

EXAM PRACTICE
Using one or two of the highlighted quotations to learn, write a paragraph exploring how Rumens presents her speaker as an outsider.

CHECKING OUT ME HISTORY
by John Agard

Dem tell me
Dem tell me
Wha dem want to tell me

Bandage up me eye with me own history
5   Blind me to me own identity

Dem tell me bout 1066 and all dat
dem tell me bout Dick Whittington and he cat
But Toussaint L'Ouverture
no dem never tell me bout dat

10   *Toussaint*
        a slave
        with vision
        lick back
        Napoleon
15   *battalion*
        and first Black
        Republic born
        Toussaint de thorn
        to de French
20   *Toussaint de beacon*
        of de Haitian Revolution

Dem tell me bout de man who discover de balloon
and de cow who jump over de moon
Dem tell me bout de dish ran away with de spoon
25   but dem never tell me bout Nanny de Maroon

Nanny
see-far woman
of mountain dream
fire-woman struggle
30   *hopeful stream*
to freedom river

Dem tell me bout Lord Nelson and Waterloo
but dem never tell me bout Shaka de great Zulu
Dem tell me bout Columbus and 1492
35   but what happen to de Caribs and de Arawaks too

Dem tell me bout Florence Nightingale and she lamp
and how Robin Hood used to camp
Dem tell me bout ole King Cole was a merry ole soul
but dem never tell me bout Mary Seacole

40   *From Jamaica*
she travel far
to the Crimean War
she volunteer to go
and even when de British said no
45   *she still brave the Russian snow*
a healing star
among the wounded
a yellow sunrise
to the dying

50   Dem tell me
Dem tell me wha dem want to tell me
But now I checking out me own history
I carving out me identity

This poem is about...

the importance of history in shaping one's identity and how a dominant white culture can make this difficult for people of non-white backgrounds.

How do the first four stanzas show the power of white culture and rebel against it?

The poet rebels against dominant culture by writing in non-standard English to reflect his Caribbean roots: dem, dat, de, wha, bout, me, he (them, that, the, what, about, my, his).

Anaphora of 'Dem tell me' is established, presenting the dominant culture as continual and oppressive. Its dominance is also shown through the contrast of plural and singular pronouns.

Two metaphors, 'Bandage up me eye with me own history / Blind me to me own identity', present the idea that the dominant culture oppresses people by only teaching white history. Ignoring the heritage of non-white people means they don't know their past and can't find their true identity. The verbs and the accompanying plosives suggest this is a form of attack.

Agard includes a reference to the Battle of Hastings, adding 'and all dat' to suggest its irrelevance to him. He also includes the folk story of Dick Whittington, choosing a minor figure linked to pantomime to contrast with more important non-white stories that genuinely merit being taught but aren't. One of these is the black military leader, Toussaint L'Ouverture, a key figure in the abolition of slavery. The speaker adds 'no dem never tell me bout dat', repeating negatives to imply anything that challenges the idea of white power is prohibited.

In defiance, the speaker provides a quick history lesson about L'Ouverture, using the colloquial verb phrase 'lick back' instead of conventional language. He describes him as a metaphorical 'thorn' and 'beacon', conveying how he fought against oppression and provided hope to others.

How do stanzas 5 and 6 develop the speaker's argument?

The speaker emphasises the idea of white history being pointless to him by sarcastically referring to the discovery of the balloon and the nonsense nursery rhyme Hey Diddle Diddle. He contrasts this irrelevance with the history of Nanny de Maroon, a Jamaican national hero who fought against British **colonialism** and freed hundreds of slaves.

Like L'Ouverture, she is linked to resistance ('fire-woman struggle'), hope ('hopeful stream') and liberty ('freedom river'). She is presented as a woman of vision ('see-far woman / of mountain dream'), linking to the speaker's earlier feelings of blindness. Agard implies these qualities are still needed today to inspire people to resist oppression by a dominant white culture.

How do the final four stanzas explore history and culture?

Stanza 7 contrasts white historical figures linked to victory and colonialism (Lord Nelson and Christopher Columbus) with black historical figures (Shaka) and the victims of colonialism (Zulu, Caribs, Arawaks). This, again, implies the importance of resisting a dominant white culture.

The references to white history become increasingly jokey as they move from Florence Nightingale to Robin Hood and another nursery rhyme, Old King Cole. As with previous stanzas, Agard then presents a non-white historical figure. Mary Seacole was a mixed-race nurse and business woman, often overshadowed by history's focus on Nightingale. She is described as generous ('volunteer') and courageous ('brave the Russian snow'), with Agard adding how she wasn't wanted then or now ('de British said no'). Metaphors linked to light ('healing star [...] yellow sunrise') present Seacole as another symbol of hope, both in her lifetime and today as proof you don't have to be white to succeed.

The speaker uses the last stanza to emphasise why non-white history is important. He repeats the opening of the poem but adds, 'now I checking out me own history / I carving out me identity'. The colloquial verb phrase suggests the importance of knowing your roots, as opposed to someone else's (as shown by the adjective 'own'). The final metaphor emphasises this idea, conveying the role of history in the construction of an individual identity.

How does the poem's form contribute to the way meaning is conveyed?

The poem uses non-standard English and ignores punctuation rules. This combines with free verse and irregular stanzas to present a rejection of poetic traditions, seen as part of the dominant white culture. It also reflects the poem's mood of freedom and criticism of restriction (represented by the different references to colonialism).

The lack of full stops, especially at the very end, also implies that nothing has been resolved: the lack of official non-white history still needs addressing.

The poet uses rhyme to highlight different images and sometimes create humour. Rhyme also represents how two types of culture are being explored by Agard: the dominant white culture and the secondary non-white culture.

The passages of non-white history are italicised and indented, linking to the image of 'carving' out an identity. This makes them stand out as well as symbolically moving them from the margin towards the centre (when something is marginalised, it is seen as unimportant whereas something central is seen as important).

Additional context to consider

John Agard was born and raised in British Guiana, a British colony in the Caribbean. When he was a teenager, the nation gained independence and became Guyana. He is a performance poet, a style that focuses on constructing language to reflect music rhythms and the patterns of everyday speech (rather than making it fit traditional forms and metres).

Although written in the first person, the poem aims to speak for any non-white person who feels marginalised by society.

Poetic links

- Empire and establishment in 'Ozymandias' or 'London'.
- The power to make others outsiders in 'The Émigrée'.
- The wish to remove power structures in 'London' or 'Tissue'.

Sample analysis

'Checking Out Me History' and 'The Émigrée' explore how people are made to feel like outsiders. Agard accuses the British establishment of creating a dominant white culture that stops non-white people from finding their place in society. The anaphora of 'dem never tell me bout' suggests non-white history is continually withheld. The adverb 'never' emphasises this absence while the contrast between plural and singular pronouns implies how this reinforces the feeling of being a minority. Linking to being a performance poet, Agard uses non-standard English and free verse to reflect his position as an outsider.

The title of Rumens's poem instantly focuses on being made an outsider. In the line 'They accuse me of absence, they circle me', she uses a similar contrast of plural and singular pronouns to Agard. The line is presented as being part of the speaker's imagination, creating a sense of the paranoia felt by an outsider. The verbs suggest feeling on trial and being outnumbered, while the use of parallelism presents this as a constant tool of oppression.

Questions

QUICK TEST
1. Why might Agard use non-standard English?
2. How did L'Ouverture resist a dominant culture?
3. What references does the poem make to colonialism?
4. How is each historical figure linked to hope?

EXAM PRACTICE
Using one or two of the highlighted quotations to learn, write a paragraph exploring how Agard presents the power of history.

KAMIKAZE by Beatrice Garland

Her father embarked at sunrise
with a flask of water, a samurai sword
in the cockpit, a shaven head
full of powerful incantations

5 and enough fuel for a one-way
journey into history

but half way there, she thought,
recounting it later to her children,
he must have looked far down

10 at the little fishing boats
strung out like bunting
on a green-blue translucent sea

and beneath them, arcing in swathes
like a huge flag waved first one way

15 then the other in a figure of eight,
the dark shoals of fishes
flashing silver as their bellies
swivelled towards the sun

and remembered how he

20 and his brothers waiting on the shore
built cairns of pearl-grey pebbles

to see whose withstood longest
the turbulent inrush of breakers
bringing their father's boat safe

25 – yes, grandfather's boat – safe
to the shore, salt-sodden, awash
with cloud-marked mackerel,
black crabs, feathery prawns,
the loose silver of whitebait and once

30 a tuna, the dark prince,
muscular, dangerous.

And though he came back
my mother never spoke again
in his presence, nor did she meet his eyes
and the neighbours too, they treated him

35 as though he no longer existed,
only we children still chattered and laughed

till gradually we too learned
to be silent, to live as though
he had never returned, that this

40 was no longer the father we loved.
And sometimes, she said, he must have wondered
which had been the better way to die.

From The Invention of Fireworks by Beatrice Garland
Published by TEMPLAR POETRY
www.templarpoetry.com   ISBN 9781906285678

This poem is about...

a Second World War kamikaze pilot who doesn't fulfil his suicide mission but returns home, only for his family to reject him.

How does the first stanza present the pilot?

The poet describes how the woman's father 'embarked at sunrise', implying someone ready and willing to die for his country. The reference to 'sunrise' symbolises how he sees glory in his mission; the metaphor 'one-way journey into history' has a slightly sarcastic tone, suggesting the speaker or the poet is challenging this idea.

References to Japanese culture present the man as an honourable soldier. A 'samurai sword' was a sign of military nobility in Japan; samurais also believed in loyalty and honour through death. A 'shaven head' was also a sign of status and was said to represent self-discipline. His 'powerful incantations' relate to the prayers of his Shinto religion, suggesting he is a devout man. However, all these references could suggest that he has been manipulated by the power structures of a strict regime into believing that dying for his country is honourable.

How do stanzas 2–5 show the pilot's change of mind?

The enjambment between the first two stanzas signals the change by creating a dramatic pause before the 'but'. The man's daughter is 'recounting' the story to her children and her tone seems calm and neutral.

The pilot is presented as seeing the beauty of his life: 'little fishing boats / strung out like bunting / on a green-blue translucent sea'. The adjective 'translucent' implies a moment of clarity, making him change his mind. The simile suggests a celebration of his peaceful life, echoed in the third stanza, 'like a huge flag'. However, bunting and flags also have connotations of nationalism, suggesting the conflict he feels between his life and his duty. These tranquil images of the sea, 'fishes / flashing silver as their bellies / swivelled towards the sun', contrast with his mission to crash into enemy boats; the sibilance in this image adds a hushed tone that could represent him considering the unspeakable act of dishonour.

He thinks of his brothers and father, and their life together. To build up an impression of his powerful desire to stay, the poet uses a list that draws on different senses: sound ('turbulent inrush'), touch ('feathery'), sight ('cloud-marked') and taste (mackerel, crab, etc.). The metaphor 'loose silver of whitebait' suggests his sudden realisation that he values this way of life, while the description of the tuna, 'dark prince, muscular, dangerous', suggests he can now see honour in the simple life of a fisherman.

How do the last two stanzas explore the consequences of his decision?

Upon his return, the man is seen as dishonoured. His wife is ashamed of him, 'never spoke again / in his presence, nor did she meet his eyes', and he is shunned by his neighbours, 'as though he no longer existed'.

The verbs 'chattered and laughed' show that only the children treat him as before. However, the enjambment signals a change in their behaviour, revealing they also grew to ignore him: 'we too learned / to be silent, to live as though / he had never returned, that this / was no longer the father we loved'. The use of the verb 'learned' emphasises the power of social judgement and political **propaganda**, linking to how the people have been manipulated into seeing kamikaze missions as good and honourable. The verb 'loved', in the past tense, suggests this manipulation is so powerful it places the state above family and emotions.

The final comment, 'he must have wondered / which had been the better way to die', highlights the sad irony of his situation: aborting his mission because he loves his family only for them to hate him; escaping death only to be treated as if he is dead. The noun phrase 'better way to die' emphasises that the man was trapped or doomed by his country's sense of duty. The verb 'wondered' also implies that he came to regret his decision.

At the end of the poem, it is still unclear what the daughter feels about her father. In the context of the last stanza, it suggests she continued to feel contempt for him and is passing on the story to her children to ensure they are always honourable. However, there is no specific criticism of her father; she could be admitting guilt for her own behaviour as her words at the end suggest sympathy and regret.

How does the poem's form contribute to the way meaning is conveyed?

For most of this narrative poem, the poet reports the words of the pilot's daughter as she talks to her children. We are also given some of her account in the first person, and stanzas 2–5 show her imagining her father's reasons for not completing his mission.

The poem is arranged in seven sestets and this set pattern contrasts with the poet's use of free verse. This could reflect the conflict the pilot experiences: follow orders and fulfil his duty or follow his heart and be with his family.

Additional context to consider

'Kamikaze' is set within a different culture to ours during the Second World War so a modern reader's values will be different to those encountered in the poem. A modern British poet may also explore the subject differently due to hindsight.

Because it is not a personal experience, the poem might also present a more objective view.

Poetic links

- Attitudes to sacrifice in 'Poppies'.
- Bravery / cowardice in 'The Charge of the Light Brigade'.
- The importance of honour in 'My Last Duchess'.
- Individuals' responses to conflict in 'Bayonet Charge', 'Poppies' or 'War Photographer'.

Sample analysis

'Kamikaze' and 'Poppies' present different views of sacrifice, partly due to each poem's different situation and cultural setting. In 'Kamikaze', the pilot doesn't fulfil his mission. His daughter is described remembering how 'we too learned / to be silent, to live as though / he had never returned', with the images of silence and death showing he was shunned for losing honour and the enjambment creating awkward pauses to convey the atmosphere around him. The adverb 'too' emphasises how everyone treated him like this while the verb 'learned' shows that, culturally, it was what was expected.

Weir's dramatic monologue is from the point of view of a mother whose son has died. Unlike 'Kamikaze', the simile 'the war memorial, / leaned against it like a wishbone' suggests a longing for her son's sacrifice to have never taken place. The wishbone image also implies that grief has brought her close to breaking point. The reference to the memorial shows that, like Garland's poem, sacrifice is linked to honour; however, it seems no consolation to the mother.

Questions

QUICK TEST

1. How is the pilot initially presented as honourable?
2. How might the 'bunting' and 'flag' similes show his conflicting feelings?
3. How might the 'translucent sea' be symbolic?
4. How do the pilot's children change when he returns?

EXAM PRACTICE

Using one or two of the highlighted quotations to learn, write a paragraph exploring how Garland presents the pilot's conflicting feelings.

How do I start to compare two poems?

You will have one poem in front of you (the one named by the examiner in the question) and will need to pick a suitable poem for comparison from your memory of the other Power and Conflict poems. The exam paper features a list of all the poem titles to help you remember.

It should be easier to find different ideas about the poem that is printed in the paper than from the one you've chosen from memory. For this reason it is a good idea to start by focusing on the poem from your memory and then link it to the poem you've been given, rather than the other way round.

In the exam you need to come up with a quick plan. If you have plenty of revision time, practise planning and writing some poetry essays. Take your time getting used to planning so, by the time it comes to the actual exam, you can do it quickly.

Begin by noting down the quotations that you've learned and thinking about how you can relate them to the exam question. What are the key ideas and the key features in each quotation? You should also consider whether the title is relevant to the question as this gives you additional language to analyse.

For example:

Compare how poets present powerful people in 'Ozymandias' and one other poem.

- 'My Last Duchess'

Shows he's a duke – importance of social position. Use of possessive pronoun.

- 'She had / A heart – how shall I say? – too soon made glad, / Too easily impressed'

Judgemental, repetition.

- 'as if she ranked / My gift of a nine-hundred-years-old name / With anybody's gift'

Social superiority, metaphor, use of 'ranked'.

- 'I choose / Never to stoop.'

Verbs: 'choose' shows freedom, 'stoop' suggests social superiority. Enjambment.

- 'This grew; I gave commands; / Then all smiles stopped together.'

'Power over servants, power of life and death, lack of remorse.

Once you've gathered your ideas about your chosen poem, decide what links you can make with the poem named by the examiner.

Add to your previous notes. If it helps, you could use a table, as this provides a visual clarification of comparisons and contrasts.

For example:

My Last Duchess	Ozymandias
1. 'My Last Duchess' Shows he's a duke – importance of social position. Use of possessive pronoun.	1. 'Ozymandias' Name of ancient Egyptian pharaoh – importance of status but also that his power has passed.
2. 'She had / A heart – how shall I say? – too soon made glad, / Too easily impressed' Judgemental, repetition.	2. 'Half sunk, a shatter'd visage lies, whose frown / And wrinkled lip and sneer of cold command' Judgemental, commanding, tricolon. Contrasts with loss of power.
3. 'as if she ranked / My gift of a nine-hundred-years-old name / With anybody's gift' Social superiority, metaphor, use of 'ranked'.	3. 'My name is Ozymandias, king of kings: / Look on my works, ye Mighty, and despair!' Superiority, imperative, sense of rank and better than God.
4. 'I choose / Never to stoop.' Verbs: 'choose' shows freedom, 'stoop' suggests social superiority. Enjambment.	4. 'And on the pedestal [...] Round the decay / Of that colossal wreck' Superiority contrasted with loss of power. Symbolism, nouns.
5. 'This grew; I gave commands; / Then all smiles stopped together.' Power over servants, power of life and death, lack of remorse.	5. 'The hand that mock'd them and the heart that fed' Bad ruler who used and exploited his people, metaphor.

You should be able to find similar or contrasting ideas in your two poems; these ideas can form sections of comparison. Look at whether your ideas run in a coherent order and, if not, rearrange them. For example, in the table above, number 2 could move after the current number 4 so the ideas about social superiority are grouped together and the ideas about commands aren't separated.

Ideally, you will have a variety of ideas. However, don't worry if some ideas are similar (as with numbers 3 and 4 above). Use opening words or phrases – such as 'Furthermore...', 'This can also be seen...' and 'Similarly...' – at the start of your paragraphs to suggest this is your way of deliberately developing your point.

While you shouldn't worry about having similar points, you should try to avoid always analysing the same literary features. The examiner wants to see a range of understanding so if every paragraph of your essay analyses metaphors they won't be impressed. Try to choose quotations that allow you different analysis and, when practising essay writing, highlight the features you're going to explore on your plan so you can make sure they are different.

How do I structure a poetry comparison?

Always start your essay with a very brief introduction. Make sure you clarify which poem you have chosen to use as comparison and try to make a statement that links to the exam question. For example:

> In 'My Last Duchess' and 'Ozymandias', Browning and Shelley present powerful people who are keen to display their superiority. However, while Browning's poem is set in the past, Shelley's poem is actually looking back on the past in order to present powerful people as having only a temporary influence.

One way of approaching the comparison is to write for 20 minutes about one poem then write for 20 minutes about your second poem. However, you must make sure that, when you write about the second poem, you keep linking your ideas back to the first. You can do this using simple opening phrases like: 'In comparison to 'My Last Duchess'...', 'Like Browning...', 'Shelley displays a similar idea to Browning when...' and 'Unlike 'My Last Duchess'...'

A much better way to write your essay is to alternate your paragraphs between the two poems:

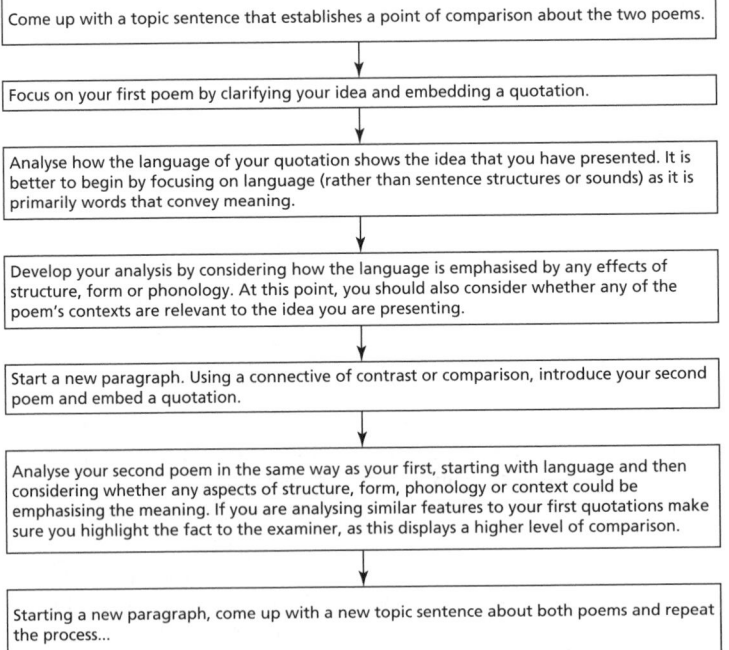

Come up with a topic sentence that establishes a point of comparison about the two poems.

Focus on your first poem by clarifying your idea and embedding a quotation.

Analyse how the language of your quotation shows the idea that you have presented. It is better to begin by focusing on language (rather than sentence structures or sounds) as it is primarily words that convey meaning.

Develop your analysis by considering how the language is emphasised by any effects of structure, form or phonology. At this point, you should also consider whether any of the poem's contexts are relevant to the idea you are presenting.

Start a new paragraph. Using a connective of contrast or comparison, introduce your second poem and embed a quotation.

Analyse your second poem in the same way as your first, starting with language and then considering whether any aspects of structure, form, phonology or context could be emphasising the meaning. If you are analysing similar features to your first quotations make sure you highlight the fact to the examiner, as this displays a higher level of comparison.

Starting a new paragraph, come up with a new topic sentence about both poems and repeat the process...

If you're feeling particularly confident in your skills of comparison and analysis, you can try to base your topic sentence round a specific poetic technique. For example: Browning and Shelley both use metaphor to show how their subjects abuse their power.

This is difficult to sustain for an entire essay so you may just include one or two sections of comparison that have this specific focus on poetic technique.

What does a good section of comparison look like?

If you look back at each of the fifteen Power and Conflict poems on pages 4–67, there is a sample section of analysis to help get you thinking about how to compare each poem.

You should try to write fairly equally about the two poems but don't worry about counting up words and making sure it's exact! Try to write in an unhurried and methodical way so you remember to include all the different elements that you need in each section of comparison.

Look at the section of analysis below and annotate it to show how it uses the flow diagram of comparison from page 70.

Browning and Shelley present their powerful people as displaying a sense of extreme superiority. In 'My Last Duchess', the Duke explains how 'I choose / Never to stoop' when discussing his complaint about his previous wife. The verbs in this line are significant as 'choose' implies personal freedom while 'stoop' shows that he sees himself as higher than other people (including his wife). As the poem is written as a dramatic monologue, Browning creates a sense of the Duke's power by him having power over his own narrative. This can be seen particularly in the enjambment, continuing the sentence into the next line in order to emphasise the word 'never' and highlight how certain he is of his superiority over others.

Similarly, Shelley shows Ozymandias's sense of superiority in the lines 'And on the pedestal [...] Round the decay / Of that colossal wreck', but contrasts it with his complete loss of power. The image of the pedestal is symbolic of him considering himself higher than others. This perhaps matches Shelley's choice of form as the sonnet, traditionally linked to love poetry, could reflect Ozymandias's self-love or hubris. However, this becomes ironic when the nouns 'decay' and 'wreck' show all that is left of his proud empire. The adjective 'colossal' is also effective as it suggests size and power yet also conveys the scale of Ozymandias's loss.

Questions

QUICK TEST
1. Are you allowed to refer to the title of the poem as part of your analysis?
2. Is it better to write one half of your essay on one poem and one half on the other poem, or alternate your paragraphs between the two poems?
3. What is the point of a topic sentence?
4. In each of your paragraphs, what aspect of the poet's writing is it better to analyse first?

EXAM PRACTICE
Looking at the table on page 69, the flow diagram on page 70 and the exemplar above, write another section of analysis comparing how poets present powerful people in 'Ozymandias' and 'My Last Duchess'.

Practice Questions

1. Compare how poets present attitudes to sacrifice in 'Kamikaze' and one other poem.

> **Notes**
>
> Kamikaze
> - sacrifice linked to honour
> - peace/family more important
> - man ostracised; ambiguous viewpoints
>
> Poppies
> - sacrifice linked to honour
> - sacrifice causes grief; difficult to convey feelings
> - mother wants him alive; honour no consolation
>
> Different cultural contexts; objective vs subjective; narrative vs lyric/elegy

2. Compare how poets explore attitudes to war in 'War Photographer' and one other poem.

> **Notes**

3. Compare the ways poets explore bravery in 'The Charge of the Light Brigade' and one other poem.

> **Notes**

4. Compare how poets depict conflict and suffering in 'Exposure' and one other poem.

> **Notes**

5. Compare the ways poets present criticism of the establishment in 'London' and one other poem.

> **Notes**

6. Compare the ways poets explore ethics during conflict in 'Remains' and one other poem.

> **Notes**

7. Compare how poets present an individual's response to conflict in 'Bayonet Charge' and one other poem.

> Notes

8. Compare how poets present attitudes to killing in 'Remains' and one other poem.

> Notes

9. Compare how poets use dramatic monologues in 'My Last Duchess' and one other poem.

> Notes

10. Compare the ways poets explore the loss of power in 'Ozymandias' and one other poem.

```
                              Notes
```

11. Compare how poets depict places experiencing conflict in 'The Émigrée' and one other poem.

```
                              Notes
```

12. Compare the ways poets explore power in 'My Last Duchess' and one other poem.

```
                              Notes
```

13. Compare the ways poets depict powerlessness in 'The Prelude' and one other poem.

Notes

14. Compare how poets explore the importance of honour in 'Kamikaze' and one other poem.

Notes

15. Compare how poets present the power of memory in 'Poppies' and one other poem.

Notes

16. Compare the ways poets explore the power to make others outsiders in 'Checking Out Me History' and one other poem.

Notes

17. Compare how poets present the wish to remove power structures in 'Tissue' and one other poem.

Notes

18. Compare how poets use imagery in 'Exposure' and one other poem.

Notes

Tips and Assessment Objectives

Quick tips

- You will get one question on the Power and Conflict poems (plus a question on the Love and Relationships poems if you have studied both collections).

- The examiner will name one poem and it will be printed for you. Read it carefully to fully refresh your memory. You will need to think of a second poem from the Power and Conflict collection that is suitable for comparison.

- Make sure you know what the question is asking you and underline the key words.

- You should spend about 45 minutes on your poetry comparison response. Allow yourself five minutes to plan your answer so there is some structure to your essay.

- All your paragraphs should contain a clear idea, a relevant reference to a poem (ideally a quotation) and analysis of how the poet conveys this idea. Your paragraphs should be linked through comparison and, when relevant, you should link your comments to the poems' contexts.

- It can sometimes help, after each paragraph, to quickly re-read the question to keep yourself focused on the exam task.

- Keep your writing concise. If you waste time 'waffling' you won't be able to include the full range of analysis and understanding that the mark scheme requires.

- It is a good idea to remember what the mark scheme is asking of you...

AO1: Understand and compare the poems (12 marks)

This is all about coming up with a range of points that match the question, supporting your ideas with references from the poems and writing your essay in a mature, academic style.

Lower	Middle	Upper
The essay has some good comparative ideas that are mostly relevant. Some quotations and references are used to support the ideas.	A clear essay that always focuses on the exam question. Quotations and references support ideas effectively. The response includes several comparisons.	A convincing, well-structured essay that answers the question fully. Quotations and references are well-chosen and integrated into sentences. The response provides a detailed and thoughtful comparison of the two poems.

AO2: Analyse effects of the poets' language, structure and form (12 marks)

You need to comment on how specific words, language techniques or sentence structures and the poetic form or metre allow the poets to get their ideas across. To achieve this, you will need to have learned good quotations to analyse.

Lower	Middle	Upper
Identification of some different methods used by the poets to convey meaning. Some subject terminology.	Explanation of the poets' different methods. Clear understanding of the effects of these methods. Accurate use of subject terminology.	Analysis of the full range of the poets' methods. Thorough exploration of the effects of these methods. Accurate range of subject terminology.

AO3: Understand the relationship between the poems and their contexts (6 marks)

For this part of the mark scheme, you need to show your understanding of how the meaning of the poems has been affected by the ways in which they have been written. You could also consider how the meaning of the poems is affected by who wrote them and when they were written.

Lower	Middle	Upper
Some awareness of how ideas are affected by the poems' contexts.	References to relevant aspects of context show a clear understanding.	Exploration is linked to specific aspects of the poems' contexts to show a detailed understanding.

Planning a Poetry Response

How might the exam question be phrased?

A typical poetry comparison question will read like this:

Compare how poets present war in 'The Charge of the Light Brigade' and one other poem. [30 marks]

How do I work out what to do?

The focus of this question is clear: the presentation of war.

'Compare' and 'how' are important elements of this question.

For AO1, 'compare' shows that you need to make a series of structured and well-developed comparisons about war in the poems. The examiner names one poem and you have to choose a second that is suitable for comparison. Only the poem named in the question will be printed for you; ideally, you should include quotations that you have learned from the other poem but, if necessary, you can make a clear reference to a specific part of the poem.

For AO2, 'how' makes it clear that you need to analyse the different ways in which the poets use language, structure and form to help to show things about war.

You also need to remember to link your comments to the poems' contexts to achieve your AO3 marks. Think about the way the poems have been written and how this has affected the ways in which meaning is conveyed.

How can I plan my essay?

You have approximately 45 minutes to write your essay.

This isn't long but you should spend the first five minutes writing a quick plan. This will help you to focus your thoughts and produce a well-structured comparative essay.

Try to come up with three or four comparisons (they can be similarities and / or differences). Each of these comparisons can then be written up as a paragraph. For more detailed advice on planning a comparison, look back at pages 68–71.

You can plan in whatever way you find most useful. Some students like to just make a quick list of points and then re-number them into a logical order. Spider diagrams are particularly popular; look at the example opposite.

'The Charge of the Light Brigade'

War = frightening and exciting

'Cannon to right of them, / Cannon to left of them, / Cannon in front of them'

'Plunged in the battery-smoke / Right thro' the line they broke'

War = full of death (but described euphemistically)

'While horse and hero fell, / [...] All that was left of them, / Left of six hundred'

*context – Tennyson celebrating the soldiers (Owen exposing the truth)

War = honourable

'When can their glory fade? / [...] Honour the charge they made!'

'Exposure'

War = frightening but not exciting; full of despair

'Sudden successive flights of bullets streak the silence'

'Less deadly than the air that shudders black with snow'

*context – Owen's personal experience in first person (Tennyson distanced – third person)

War = full of death (described vividly)

'Tonight, His frost will fasten on this mud and us, / Shrivelling many hand, puckering foreheads crisp'

War = degrading and hopeless

'We cringe in holes'

'Pause over half-known faces. All their eyes are ice, / But nothing happens'

Presentation of war

Summary

- Make sure you know what the focus of the essay is.
- Remember to compare the two poems.
- Remember to analyse how ideas are conveyed by each poet.
- Try to relate your ideas to the poems' contexts.

Questions

QUICK TEST

1. What key skills do you need to show in your answer?
2. What are the benefits of quickly planning your essay?
3. Why is it better to have learned quotations for the exam?

EXAM PRACTICE

Plan a response to the following exam question:

Compare how poets present the power of nature in 'Storm on the Island' and one other poem.

[30 marks]

Grade 5 Annotated Response

Compare how poets present war in 'The Charge of the Light Brigade' and one other poem.

[30 marks]

'The Charge of the Light Brigade' and 'Exposure' present different views of war (1).

Both poems present war as frightening: 'Cannon to right of them, / Cannon to left of them, / Cannon in front of them'. The word 'cannon' links to danger and it is repeated three times to show the soldiers are surrounded by danger (2). The rhythm of the poem and its short lines make the poem quick to read so the battle sounds exciting. This can also be seen in the descriptions of fighting: 'Plunged in the battery-smoke / Right thro' the line they broke'. The verbs sound very strong and powerful and this is added to by the plosive sounds (3).

In comparison, Owen's poem also presents war as frightening. 'Sudden successive flights of bullets streak the silence' is a short sentence. The word 'sudden' shows the men are scared because something has suddenly happened and this would make them frightened (4). The quotations also use sibilance; these sounds sound like a snake hissing so it makes the bullets sound dangerous because it sounds like they're attacking. Owen's poem is depressing because it focuses on the conditions. This might be because Owen was a soldier whereas Tennyson wasn't so they focus on different parts of war. He describes it as really cold and even the snow is described as being black as if everything is miserable and hopeless (5).

Tennyson describes the deaths of the soldiers: 'While horse and hero fell, / They that had fought so well / Came thro' the jaws of Death / Back from the mouth of Hell, / All that was left of them, / Left of six hundred'. The verb 'fell' doesn't sound painful or scary. It sounds clean and quick and is linked to being a 'hero'. Repeating the word 'left' shows that lots of soldiers died but focuses more on survival because he wanted to celebrate the brave deeds of the Light Brigade (6).

Owen's poem shows how horrible the war was (7). The deaths of the soldiers sound horrible. 'Tonight, His frost will fasten on this mud and us, / Shrivelling many hands, puckering foreheads crisp' sounds horrible because of the last two verbs. Also, they die in 'mud', which suggests they are beaten and feel worthless. The word 'many' shows that lots of people died, which is similar to when Tennyson writes about not many soldiers being 'left' (8).

Tennyson presents war as honourable. The last stanza, 'When can their glory fade? / O the wild charge they made! / All the world wonder'd. / Honour the charge they made!', makes the men sound as if they have achieved greatness by dying in the war. This is shown by the words 'glory' and 'honour'. Tennyson uses a rhetorical question and an imperative. This shows the men's deaths are important (9).

In comparison, Owen presents war as not being glorious at all (10). In the poem he describes the men hiding in holes, which makes them sound like animals rather than honourable men. Owen isn't criticising them, he is showing how bad the war is. He compares the soldiers' eyes to ice which shows how they were left to die of hypothermia which contrasts with the idea of being respected in Tennyson's poem (11). As well as describing the dead soldiers it could show that the burial party are emotionless because they have seen so much death and know it might be their turn soon. This also suggests that war is horrible rather than honourable.

1. Clear introduction showing which other poem is being used for comparison. The student could identify how the poems are different in order to establish an argument or exploration. AO1

2. Clear point, evidence and analysis. However, the quotation could be embedded, the expression considered more and subject terminology more sophisticated. AO2

3. Fairly good attempt to develop analysis through form and phonology but understanding could be stronger. AO2

4. A connective is used to clarify comparison. Good choice of quotation but not embedded. Some good analysis but writing could be more concise and precise. Some evidence of feature spotting with the reference to the short sentence. AO1/AO2

5. Good development of analysis and some brief consideration of context. AO2/AO3

6. Good analysis, although expression could be more precise. Quotation is too long; not all of it is analysed. Some use of context when considering Tennyson's aim and tone. AO2/AO1/AO3

7. Although comparison is implied, the student needs to make it clear to the examiner. The repetition of 'horrible' in this paragraph is vague and clumsy. AO1/AO2

8. Some good close comparison. AO1/AO2

9. Quotation is embedded but it is too long; not all of it is analysed. There is some feature spotting of structural techniques. AO1/AO2

10. Some good comparison but the connective could be varied. Overall, comparison has been quite simple and mechanical. AO1

11. This sentence is poorly constructed. The student would benefit from another quotation from 'Exposure' so comments are analytical rather than general. AO2

Questions

EXAM PRACTICE

Choose a paragraph of this essay. Read it through a few times then try to rewrite and improve it. You might:

- improve the sophistication of the language or the clarity of expression .
- replace a reference with a quotation or use a better quotation
- ensure quotations are embedded in the sentence
- provide more detailed, or a wider range of, analysis
- use subject terminology more effectively
- link some context to the analysis more effectively.

Grade 7+ Annotated Response

A proportion of the best top-band answers will be awarded Grade 8 or Grade 9. To achieve this, you should aim for a sophisticated, fluid and nuanced response that displays flair and originality.

Compare how poets present war in 'The Charge of the Light Brigade' and one other poem. [30 marks]

'The Charge of the Light Brigade' presents a more traditional and patriotic view of war than 'Exposure' which, linking to the title's suggestion of revealing truth, focuses on the reality of the soldiers' suffering (1).

Both poems present war as frightening. Tennyson repeats the tricolon, 'Cannon to right of them, / Cannon to left of them, / Cannon in front of them', to present the soldiers as surrounded by danger. The use of dactylic dimeter stresses the cannons and their placement but the short lines and their regular rhythm also create a sense of excitement in battle. This can also be seen in the descriptions of fighting, 'Plunged in the battery-smoke / Right thro' the line they broke', where the powerful verbs convey courageous actions that are emphasised by the plosive sounds (2).

Owen's poem also presents war as frightening but shows no excitement (3). The short dramatic sentence, 'Sudden successive flights of bullets streak the silence', uses the adjective 'sudden' to suggest the men's fear but also reminds the reader that the poem is about waiting rather than action. The sibilance creates a tone of danger while also mirroring the sound of the bullets to increase the reader's empathy. Owen adds a greater sense of despair, perhaps because – unlike Tennyson's poem – this describes a personal experience, heightened by the use of the first person rather than the more distanced third person (4). Adding that bullets are 'Less deadly than the air that shudders black with snow' is a surprising line that uses metaphor to convey the terrible conditions. The colour 'black' symbolises a lack of hope that is deepened through its association with snow, something usually linked to whiteness and purity.

Both poems present the death of soldiers but Tennyson's writing is more euphemistic. In the lines 'While horse and hero fell / [...] All that was left of them, / Left of six hundred', the verb 'fell' presents death as clean and quick. It is linked directly to heroism but, although the repetition of 'left' alludes to the amount of deaths, Tennyson focuses more on survival. This suggests he was seeking to celebrate the brave deeds of the Light Brigade (5).

Owen's poem, however, seeks to expose the full horror of war. Death is described in a much more vivid way, 'Tonight, His frost will fasten on this mud and us, / Shrivelling many hands, puckering foreheads crisp', with the last two verbs focusing on gruesome physical effects. Their deaths in the 'mud', and the way the mud and the soldiers are presented as the same, seems far less heroic than in Tennyson's poem. The use of future tense, 'will', creates a poignant fatalism while the implication that their deaths are sent by God (through the capitalisation of His) adds a sense of utter abandonment rather than celebration (6).

Tennyson ends his poem by presenting war as honourable. The abstract noun in 'When can their glory fade? / [...] Honour the charge they made!' suggests the men have achieved lasting greatness and this is heightened by the rhetorical question. The subsequent imperative urges the reader to 'honour' the men and focuses on a sense of *success, 'their charge', rather than failure. Only the continual fall of the dactylic dimeter implies the loss of war and suggests an uncertainty about whether such slaughter is worthwhile (7).*

In contrast, Owen presents war as humiliating, using images like 'we cringe in holes' to suggest the men are reduced to animals. Rather than their deaths bringing honour, the men are barely recognised. Owen describes how the burial party 'Pause over half-known faces. All their eyes are ice, / But nothing happens', suggesting that so many people are dying no one knows who they are. The metaphor presents the eyes of the dead but could equally describe the lack of emotion in the other soldiers, perhaps implying they know the same fate awaits them. The final line alludes to the way the war seems never-ending, suggesting that the men have been forgotten about and left to die (8).

1. Clear introduction, establishing a sense of comparison and argument. AO1

2. Good paragraph of analysis, using embedded quotations and providing sophisticated analysis of language, form and phonology. A range of subject terminology is applied accurately. AO2

3. Clear sense of comparison. AO1

4. Good use of context, firmly linked to the surrounding analysis. AO3

5. Some sophisticated language choices. Good use of context, although it could be developed further. AO1/AO3

6. Sophisticated language use. Detailed and fluid, rather than simple and mechanical, comparison. AO1

7. Range of analysis strengthened by exploring the effects of structure and form. AO2

8. The essay has displayed consistently strong and varied analysis, detailed comparison, sophisticated language choices and clear consideration of context. AO2/AO1/AO3

Questions

EXAM PRACTICE

Spend 45 minutes writing an answer to the following question:
Compare how poets present the power of nature in 'Storm on the Island' and one other poem. [30 marks]
Remember to use the plan you have already prepared.

Glossary

Glossary of literary terms

Abstract noun – an idea or feeling rather than an object

Adjective – a word to describe a noun

Adverb – a word to describe a verb

Alliteration – a series of words beginning with the same sound

Allusion – a reference to something without specifically stating it

Anaphora – repeating words or phrases in a structured way (such as at the start of stanzas)

Caesura – a pause within a line of poetry, created by a punctuation mark

Clauses – grammatical units (sets of words) forming part of a sentence and separated by punctuation

Colloquial – everyday, informal language

Compound adjective – two words joined together by a hyphen to create an adjective

Determiner – a word that clarifies a noun, such as the, my or this

Direct speech – the actual words of a speaker, usually placed between speech marks

Dramatic monologue – a poem in which the poet adopts the voice, or persona, of a character and addresses an imagined audience

Elegy – a poem of serious reflection, often focusing on grief about death

Ellipsis – punctuation (...) used to miss out words

End-stopped – using punctuation (such as a comma, full stop or dash) at the end of a line of poetry

Enjambment – continuing a sentence across lines of poetry without end-stopping

Euphemism – replacing a harsh or taboo word or phrase with a milder, more indirect one

Exclamative sentence – a sentence that conveys strong emotion

Extended metaphor – a metaphor that is continued throughout a series of images

Figurative language – describing through comparison (simile, metaphor, personification, symbolism)

First person – using I (singular) or we (plural) to show a personal or shared experience

Foreshadowing – suggesting something that is going to happen later

Half-rhyme – a near rhyme, needing one vowel sound to change to achieve a full rhyme

Hyperbole – exaggerated language

Imperative – a sentence or word that contains an order

Internal rhyme – words that rhyme within lines of poetry (rather than at the ends of lines)

Irony – saying one thing in order to deliberately suggest the opposite; a situation that appears deliberately the opposite of what you might expect

Juxtaposition – placing two things next to each other, usually to create a contrast

Laterals – sounds (often soft) created by placing the tip of the tongue against the roof of the mouth

Lexical field – a series of words relating to a specific topic

Metaphor – a descriptive technique, using comparison to say one thing is something else

Modal verb – a verb showing the necessity or possibility of another verb (such as *could* eat, *should* eat, *might* eat)

Mood – the dominant emotion or atmosphere of a piece of writing

Nonet – a stanza consisting of nine lines

Noun – a word indicating an object

Noun phrase – a series of words making up a noun

Octave – a stanza consisting of eight lines

Onomatopoeia – words that sound like the sound they are describing

Oxymoron – a phrase created by words with apparently opposite meanings

Parallelism – repetition of a grammatical structure (often with one small change) for effect

Personification – describing an object or idea as if it has human characteristics

Phonology – sounds within speech

Plosives – harsh sounds formed through a sudden release of air from the mouth

Pronoun – words used as substitutes for nouns; personal pronouns show who is speaking (I, he, she, they); possessive pronouns indicate ownership (my, her, their); singular and plural pronouns indicate whether one or more person is involved (I/they)

Proper noun – a name of a person, place, organisation, etc.

Quatrain – a stanza consisting of four lines

Refrain – a line or series of lines repeated in a poem

Register – the level of someone's vocabulary (its complexity, variety and formality)

Repetition – saying something more than once to achieve a specific effect

Rhetorical question – a question used to make the listener think, rather than gain an answer

Rhyme – words with the same sound (patterns of rhyme can be noted using letters, so *abab* shows that the first and third lines of a poem rhyme, as do the second and fourth lines)

Second person – writing using the pronoun 'you' (as opposed to first or third person)

Sestet – a stanza consisting of six lines

Sibilance – repetition of s sounds

Simile – a descriptive technique, using like or as to form a comparison

Sonnet – a hyphenate these words poem in iambic pentameter with a fixed rhyme scheme, usually focusing on love

Stanza – a group of lines in a poem (like a paragraph of poetry)

Symbol – an object or colour used to represent a different meaning

Third person – writing using the pronouns he, she or they (as opposed to first person, I)

Tone – the way words suggest a particular mood or feeling

Tricolon – ideas or words arranged into a pattern of three for a specific effect

Verb – a doing or action word

Verb phrase – a series of words making up a verb

Vowel sounds – the sounds created when pronouncing vowels; these can be short (a, e, i, o, u) or long (A, E, I, O, U, OO, AH)

Wordplay – exploiting the ambiguous meanings of words

Metre

Metre – the rhythmic structure of a line of poetry, based on patterns of stress, created through the type and number of metrical feet it contains; if a line uses two feet it is dimeter, three feet is trimeter, four feet is tetrameter, five is pentameter, six is hexameter, etc.

Iamb – this is the most regularly used metrical foot; it consists of an unstressed beat followed by a stressed beat

Iambic pentameter – a line consisting of five iambs

Dactyl – a metrical foot consisting of a stressed beat followed by two unstressed beats

Dactylic dimeter – a line consisting of two dactyls

Spondee – a metrical foot consisting of two stressed beats

Trochee – a metrical foot consisting of a stressed beat followed by an unstressed beat

Blank verse – a poem that uses a specific metre (often iambic pentameter) but doesn't use a set rhyme scheme

Free verse – a poem that uses neither a specific metre nor a set rhyme scheme

General glossary

Ambiguous – unclear, open to interpretation

Arrogance – thinking that you are better or more important than others

Atrocity – an extreme act of violence, usually on a large scale

Capitalism – an economic system based on individual profit

Colonialism – taking control of a country in order to exploit its people and resources

Commodity – a product for sale

Conflate – combine

Corrupt – being dishonest, usually for monetary gain

Desensitised – experiencing less of an emotional reaction to powerful events

Discord – disagreement, lack of harmony

Duality – the quality of being double

Elfin – very small

Empire – a number of countries ruled over by one state or monarch

Epitaph – words written to commemorate someone's death

Establishment – the elements of society that exercise power and control

Exile – being sent away from your own country

French Revolution – social and political upheaval in France at the end of the 18th century, including the execution of the royal family

Hierarchy – a system that ranks status

Hubris – excessive pride

Idealised – an unrealistically perfect view of something

Idiom – a familiar phrase or saying

Industrial Revolution – the period, from 1760 to around 1830, when Britain changed to mechanised manufacturing processes

Light cavalry – lightly armed troops on horses

Monarchy – the royal family

Nobility – belonging to the aristocracy, a country's highest social class

Nostalgia – viewing the past in an overly positive way

Oppressive – treating people harshly in order to control them

Pall – a cloth spread over a coffin

Patriarchy – a system in which men hold power

Patriotic – strongly supporting your country

Pharaoh – an ancient Egyptian ruler

Pinnace – a boat

Poet laureate – the country's official poet, appointed by royalty

Power structures – systems and organisations that hold power and influence society

Propaganda – biased information used to promote a specific view and manipulate people

Regime – a strict government that reduces individual freedom

Remorse – regret

Sombre – serious and sad; gloomy

Surreal – dreamlike and strange

Transient – lasting only a short time

Unequivocal – definite

Unfathomable – impossible to understand

Victorian – the period of British history relating to the reign of Queen Victoria (1837–1901)

Answers

Pages 4–7: 'Ozymandias'

QUICK TEST

1. The vast legs of stone; the superior expression carved into the face; the pedestal and its inscription.
2. It is trunkless (no body); the head is shattered and half sunk in the sand; it is described as a wreck.
3. Time and the idea that nothing lasts forever.
4. It asks people to look on Ozymandias's empire and be impressed but there is nothing left to see.

EXAM PRACTICE

Ideas might include how the adjectives describing the broken statue contrast with the tricolon of dominance used to describe its face, or the use of symbolism when describing the desert and the nouns describing the statue.

Pages 8–11: 'London'

QUICK TEST

1. It emphasises the amount of weakness and misery in London, suggesting it affects everyone.
2. People are enchained by their own beliefs; people haven't been taught to value freedom; some people are considered less important in the minds of those running the country.
3. The image of putting a pall over the church suggests it could be rejected (left to die) by the population; the image of blood running down palace walls is an allusion to the execution of the royal family during the French Revolution, suggesting the same could happen in England.
4. She is young; the use of the word 'curse' suggests she has ended up as a prostitute due to misfortune.

EXAM PRACTICE

Ideas might include the repetition of 'marks' to show physical and emotional damage, emphasised by the accompanying abstract nouns; the different interpretations of the manacles metaphor; and the mistreatment of children being linked, through symbolism, to sin.

Pages 12–16: 'The Prelude'

QUICK TEST

1. Little; her; elfin pinnace; like a swan.
2. Stealing the boat; rowing it skilfully; being alone on the lake with no restrictions.
3. The size of the mountain peak, showing him his insignificance in the world.
4. The power of nature; God.

EXAM PRACTICE

Ideas might include the repetition of the adjective 'huge' and the use of colour symbolism; personification and use of powerful verbs; and the metaphor to suggest that this powerful force has affected the way he sees the world.

Pages 17–21: 'My Last Duchess'

QUICK TEST

1. Proper nouns of artists and sculptors; using the verb 'durst'; lots of first person pronouns; boasting about his 'nine-hundred-years-old name'.
2. Using the word 'dies' when referring to Frà Pandolf's description of his wife's blushes.

3. 'But I'; 'ranked my gift'; 'here you miss, or there exceed the mark'; 'choose never to stoop'; 'commands'; 'will't please you rise'.
4. The statue is symbolic of wealth (it is bronze and the sculptor is specifically named as if he is famous). It depicts Neptune, a god, which symbolises how the Duke also sees himself as godlike, with the power to choose who lives and dies. Neptune is 'Taming a sea-horse', linking to the Duke's wish to control his wife.

EXAM PRACTICE
Ideas might include how the repetition of 'too' suggests his wife didn't meet his high standards; the 'gift' metaphor suggesting the importance of an established family, linked to the verb 'ranked'; the verb 'stoop' shows he considers himself above, others; the abstract noun 'commands' show power as does the euphemism for having his wife killed.

Pages 22–25: 'The Charge of the Light Brigade'

QUICK TEST
1. Repetition of the metaphor 'valley of Death'.
2. The opening tricolon; the imperative verbs of the commander's direct speech; and the way the dactylic dimeter opens each line with a powerful stressed beat.
3. The 'Cannons' tricolon; powerful verbs of attack; directions to show the men are almost surrounded; personification of Death and Hell; and the use of phonology and structure to connect words in order to imply the enemy attack is without respite.
4. Honourable and brave/valiant

EXAM PRACTICE
Ideas might include the 'valley of Death' metaphor to show the men are being courageous, as well as the verbs suggesting brave deeds; directions and verbs present the danger the men are in; personification of Death and Hell shows what the men have faced; descriptions of their actions combined with the abstract noun 'glory', the effect of the verb 'wondered', and the rhetorical question and imperative.

Pages 26–30: 'Exposure'

QUICK TEST
1. Brutal and cold, as if it is constantly attacking them; it is shown to be deadly and there is a suggestion that it causes the soldiers to lose faith in God.
2. Personification.
3. As well as sight, there is touch and sound.
4. They know they are dying and don't expect to return home.

EXAM PRACTICE
Ideas might include the use of maddening sounds linked to death; the tricolon to emphasise the continually bad conditions; the personification of snow to suggest it is trying to kill the men; their realisation that they are going to die because of the terrible conditions rather than the fighting.

Pages 31–34: 'Storm on the Island'

QUICK TEST
1. Prepared, squat, walls, rock, good slate; plus the joke about the state of the earth.
2. Fear.
3. Pummels, exploding, hits, spits, savage, strafes, salvo, bombarded.
4. Warfare.

EXAM PRACTICE

Ideas might include how the opening line and the adjective 'prepared' suggest something bad is going to happen; the verbs 'pummels' and 'fear' show how fierce the wind is and how it makes people feel; the simile suggests the weather is wild and uncontrollable; metaphors are used to compare the wind to a military attack.

Pages 35–38: 'Bayonet Charge'

QUICK TEST

1. Opening in media res with the adverb 'suddenly'; using enjambment and a single sentence for the first 11 lines so there are fewer pauses; verbs like 'running' and 'stumbling'.
2. The rhetorical question about fate and death; the abstract noun 'bewilderment'; the surreal simile in which he freezes 'mid-stride'.
3. The hare also seems trapped (the circle); it seems innocent and scared (linking to images like the soldier's 'patriotic tear').
4. Men are turned into weapons; there is no time for values (such as patriotism and honour), it is just about killing and surviving.

EXAM PRACTICE

Ideas might include that the opening line, and the use of the adverb 'suddenly, drops the reader straight into battle to create a mood of urgency and fear; the metaphor and plosives that describe the bullets make the gunfire frightening; the list of values that are 'dropped' makes war sound simply about survival while the noun phrase 'yelling alarm' emphasises the idea of being overtaken by sheer terror.

Pages 39–42: 'Remains'

QUICK TEST

1. It makes the speaker more realistic and suggests that the killing wasn't out of the ordinary.
2. All letting fly; rips through his life; so we've hit this looter a dozen times; sort of inside out; tosses his guts; carted off.
3. Tricolon.
4. Won't flush him out.

EXAM PRACTICE

Ideas might include the way the killing is described in an excited, impressed way; the disregard for human life shown in the careless verb 'tosses'; the metaphor 'bloody hands' showing he feels guilt for what he's done.

Pages 43–46: 'Poppies'

QUICK TEST

1. Needlework.
2. Poppies are a symbol of remembrance; the 'spasms of red' suggest bleeding; the 'blockade' could link to one of his responsibilities as a soldier.
3. Blockade, bandaged, rounded up, steeled, flattened, reinforcements.
4. Steeled the softening of my face; I wanted / I resisted; I was brave; threw it open.

EXAM PRACTICE

Ideas might include the contrast of safety and danger in the flower (with its suggestions of blood) and the school blazer (that is linked to a military operation); metaphor to show she's hiding her emotions, for his benefit and to keep herself under control; metaphor to show her inability to express her feelings to her son; metaphor for her grief, either at losing her son or thinking that she might.

Pages 47–50: 'War Photographer'

QUICK TEST

1. It creates a sombre tone, shows the atrocities of war, and indicates the war photographer's detached, methodical approach to his work.
2. Softly, rural England, ordinary pain which simple weather can dispel, fields which don't explode.
3. Must.
4. It's only temporary; people have become desensitised to images of war.

EXAM PRACTICE

Ideas might include the description linking the camera film to death, the blood symbolism, the photographer's dispassionate but respectful attitude; images of war and pain contrasted with the photographer's own safe and peaceful lifestyle; the imperative showing his belief in the significance of his job, compared with the short-term effect on the newspaper readers who see his photographs then resume their daily lives.

Pages 51–54: 'Tissue'

QUICK TEST

1. Extended metaphor.
2. Could, might.
3. Experience, faith, history, family and remembrance.
4. Borderlines, credit cards, capitals, monoliths, pride.

EXAM PRACTICE

Ideas could include the extended tissue metaphor linking to transparency rather than secrets and the modal verb 'could' displaying a hope for change; the metaphor for borders and structures being erased suggests a wish for people to see themselves as global citizens; the metaphor presents the destruction of powerful establishments and ideologies, while suggesting hope being brought to people.

Pages 55–58: 'The Émigrée'

QUICK TEST

1. When she was a child.
2. Tanks, banned by the state.
3. It is a metaphor, suggesting she is not free to travel back to that country.
4. Each ends with 'sunlight' and a full stop, contrasting an image of hope or goodness with a representation of restriction.

EXAM PRACTICE

Ideas might include how the use of past tense presents the speaker as trapped in the past or living without roots; personification and simile suggest that war and political change have cut her off from her homeland; the contrast of pronouns (they/me) suggest being outnumbered; the images of death and darkness imply her homeland has become a bad place and she wouldn't be welcome or safe there.

Pages 59–63: 'Checking Out Me History'

QUICK TEST

1. To emphasise his Caribbean roots and rebel against the idea of a dominant culture.
2. He fought against slavery.
3. The Haitian Revolution, Nanny de Maroon, Lord Nelson, Zulu, Caribs, Arawaks.

4. 'Toussaint de beacon', 'hopeful stream to freedom river', 'a yellow sunrise'; these figures provided hope in the past and can still be used to provide hope to non-white people today.

EXAM PRACTICE

Ideas might include how the metaphor suggests a dominant white history has stopped him seeing who he really is; the repetition of 'dem never tell me bout' highlights the idea that history can be used as a form of oppression; history allows people to understand their own life and background and the verb 'carving' suggests this is hard work but has a long-lasting effect.

Pages 64–67: 'Kamikaze'

QUICK TEST

1. The image of 'sunrise' and glory; the cultural allusions to honour (samurai sword, shaven head, powerful incantations).
2. The similes celebrate his normal life and make him want to stay but they also link to nationalism and his duty.
3. It represents a moment of clarity as he realises he doesn't want to die.
4. At first they behave normally ('chattered and laughed') then they pick up on how everyone else treats their father and stop acknowledging his presence ('this / was no longer the father we loved').

EXAM PRACTICE

Ideas might include how the bunting simile could represent a celebration of his simple life and a reminder of his national duty; the whitebait metaphor shows he values his life more than his mission; the sad irony of the last line shows that he would have lost whichever decision he made, while the

verb 'wondered' implies he may have regretted his decision.

Pages 68–71: How to Compare Poetry

QUICK TEST

1. Yes, the title can provide you with extra language to analyse.
2. Alternate paragraphs.
3. It establishes a point of comparison about the poems, showing the examiner that you are meeting the assessment criteria.
4. Start by focusing on language then consider how meaning is emphasised by structure, form or phonology.

EXAM PRACTICE

Use the flow diagram on page 70 to check that your section follows the comparison structure.

Pages 76–77: Planning a Poetry Response

QUICK TEST

1. Comparison of the two poems, specific analysis and terminology, awareness of the relevance of context, a well-structured essay.
2. Planning focuses your thoughts and allows you to produce a well-structured essay.
3. Quotations give you more opportunities to do specific AO2 analysis.

EXAM PRACTICE

Poem choices for comparison would include 'Exposure' or 'The Prelude'. Ideas for the comparison might include what element of nature is being described as powerful, how that element is presented as powerful, what the element of nature does to people, and how people feel about or respond to the power of nature.

Pages 78–81: Graded Responses

EXAM PRACTICE

Use the mark scheme to self-assess your strengths and weaknesses. Work up from the bottom, putting a tick by things you have fully accomplished, a ½ by skills that are in place but need securing, and underlining areas that need particular development. The estimated grade boundaries are included so you can assess your progress towards your target grade.

Grade	AO1 (12 marks)	AO2 (12 marks)	AO3 (6 marks)
6–7+	A convincing, well-structured essay that answers the question fully. Quotations and references are well-chosen and integrated into sentences. The response provides a detailed and thoughtful comparison of the two poems.	Analysis of the full range of the poets' methods. Thorough exploration of the effects of these methods. Accurate range of subject terminology.	Exploration is linked to specific aspects of the poems' contexts to show a detailed understanding.
4–5	A clear essay that always focuses on the exam question. Quotations and references support ideas effectively. The response includes several comparisons.	Explanation of the poets' different methods. Clear understanding of the effects of these methods. Accurate use of subject terminology.	References to relevant aspects of context show a clear understanding.
2–3	The essay has some good comparative ideas that are mostly relevant. Some quotations and references are used to support the ideas.	Identification of some different methods used by the poets to convey meaning. Some subject terminology.	Some awareness of how ideas are affected by the poems' contexts.

THIS PAGE HAS INTENTIONALLY
BEEN LEFT BLANK